Asset Tokenization. Tokenizing the Sun

HandBook for Professionals Series

IT CAMPUS ACADEMY

MICHAEL CATHAL

Copyright © 2023 Michael Cathal

¡WELCOME TO ASSET TOKENIZATION!

The digital age has been synonymous with innovation, blurring boundaries, and expanding horizons. From the internet's expansive web connecting people across continents to artificial intelligence offering a glimpse into the potential of human-machine collaboration, each wave of technological evolution has transformed our lives in unforeseen ways. Among these seismic shifts, the concept of tokenization stands as one of the most revolutionary.

In this book, we embark on an illuminating journey into the realm of tokenized assets—a domain where the tangible meets the intangible, the ancient traditions of trade meet the futuristic brilliance of blockchain, and assets as grand and luminous as the sun can be fractionally owned, traded, and appreciated in the palm of our hand.

Tokenization, at its core, is a radical reimagination of ownership and value. By converting rights to an asset into a digital token on a blockchain, we not only simplify transactions but also democratize access to assets previously reserved for the elite. This book is not merely an exploration of this transformation but also a guidebook, a primer, and a visionary look into the possibilities that lie ahead.

From understanding the intricacies of blockchain technology to delving deep into the ethics, challenges, and potential of tokenizing everything from art to real estate, and yes, even the energy of the sun, this book serves as a beacon for beginners and experts alike. We'll navigate through the technicalities, address the skeptics, highlight the success stories, and equip you with the knowledge to discern hype from genuine innovation.

The promise of tokenization is vast, but so are the challenges. As we stand at the brink of this new frontier, this book aims to enlighten, educate, and inspire. By tokenizing assets, we're not just redefining value; we're reshaping the very fabric of our financial and social systems.

So, whether you're a seasoned tech enthusiast, a financial professional, or simply curious about the next big thing in the digital world, this book is your compass. Join us on this exploration, as we venture into a future where the digital and physical seamlessly intertwine, unlocking possibilities, potential, and a world of promise.

¡Go!

1. Introduction to the World of Tokens 10

    1.1 Definition of Tokens...10

    1.2 Types of Tokens 14

    1.3 Historical Overview 19

2. Understanding Asset Tokenization 25

    2.1 Tokenization of Real Assets 25

    2.2 Legal and Regulatory Framework 30

    2.3 Technical Aspects and Standards........................35

    2.4 Market Dynamics and Ecosystem 40

    2.5 Use Cases and Real-World Applications 44

    2.6 Regulatory and Legal Considerations..................50

    2.7 Risks and Mitigation Strategies...........................55

    2.8 Future Perspectives and Trends..........................59

3. Business Applications and Case Studies 65

   3.1 Tokenization in Various Industries 65

   3.2 Strategies and Methodologies for Tokenization .69

   3.3 Challenges, Risks, and Ethical Considerations 74

   3.4 Real-World Applications and Case Studies 78

   3.5 Future Prospects, Emerging Trends, and Innovation 83

4. Tokenizing Real Estate 88

   4.1 International and National Regulatory Frameworks 88

   4.2 Legal Considerations and Case Law 92

   4.3 Token Creation, Deployment, and Management 96

   4.4 Tokenization in Different Sectors and Industries 101

   4.5 Legal and Regulatory Compliance in Tokenization 105

4.6 Tokenization Technology: Platforms, Protocols, and Mechanisms 110

4.7 Market Dynamics, Trends, and Strategies in Tokenization 115

4.8 Legal and Regulatory Considerations in Tokenization 120

4.9 Practical Implementations of Tokenization in Various Industries 124

4.10 Challenges and Limitations of Tokenization ...129

4.11 Future Trends and Developments in Tokenization 134

4.12 Practical Considerations in Tokenizing Assets 139

4.13 Risks and Challenges in Tokenizing Assets 144

Solar Energy Tokenization Project 149

1.1 Choice of Blockchain 150

1.2 Protocol Development 150

1.3 Smart Contract Development 151

Project Implementation 153

2.1 Installation of Measurement Equipment 153

2.2 Integration of Measurement Equipment with the Blockchain Platform 153

2.3 Testing and Commissioning 154

2.4 Development of a User Interface 155

Operation and Maintenance 156

3.1 Monitoring Solar Energy Production 156

3.2 Maintenance of the Blockchain Platform 156

3.3 User Support 157

Expansion 158

Minimum Necessary Smart Contracts 159

Monetization of a Tokenization Project 170

Asset Tokenization. Tokenizing the Sun

1. Introduction to the World of Tokens

1.1 Definition of Tokens

In the digital age, the concept of tokens has become a cornerstone of various technological advancements, especially in the fields of blockchain and cryptocurrency. A token is a digital or virtual representation of ownership or rights managed on a blockchain. The word "token" signifies something that serves as a visible or tangible representation of a fact, quality, feeling, etc. Here, we'll explore the concept of tokens in detail, their essence, significance, and applications.

What Are Tokens?

Tokens are digital assets that can be bought, sold, or traded. In the world of blockchain, tokens often represent a unit of value issued by a project. Unlike cryptocurrency, which is a medium of exchange like traditional currencies, tokens often provide access to a specific application or service within a broader ecosystem.

Example: Imagine a digital marketplace where users buy tokens issued by the platform. These tokens can be used to purchase services within the platform, participate in the platform's governance, or be traded on various exchanges.

Differentiating Tokens from Coins

Tokens are often confused with coins, but there's a distinction:

- **Coins**: These are native to their own blockchain (e.g., Bitcoin on the Bitcoin blockchain).
- **Tokens**: These are created on existing blockchains (e.g., an ERC-20 token on the Ethereum blockchain).

Example: Bitcoin (BTC) is a coin, whereas USD Tether (USDT) is a token running on different blockchains including Ethereum and Binance Smart Chain.

Functional Representation

Tokens can represent anything from physical objects to agreements and rights:

- **Access Rights**: Tokens can grant holders the right to use a specific service within an ecosystem.
- **Asset Ownership**: Tokens can signify ownership in an asset, such as real estate or artwork.
- **Governance Rights**: Some tokens allow holders to participate in decision-making processes within a decentralized organization.

Example: The governance token of a decentralized finance (DeFi) platform may allow token holders to vote on updates, changes, or directions for the platform.

Creation and Management

Tokens are usually created through smart contracts on existing blockchains like Ethereum, Binance Smart Chain, etc. The creation involves defining the rules, total supply, and functionalities of the token.

Example: An organization may decide to issue a token with a total supply of 1 million, where each token represents a share in the company. These tokens can be bought, sold, or held for dividend rights.

Tokens in the Real World

The application of tokens extends beyond the virtual world. Physical assets, agreements, and rights can also be tokenized, allowing for decentralized ownership and trade.

Example: A piece of art can be tokenized into 1000 tokens, where each token represents 0.1% ownership in the art piece. Token holders can trade their shares or hold them as investment.

Conclusion

The definition of tokens captures a versatile and dynamic concept that transcends traditional boundaries. As digital representations, tokens are a means to democratize access, ownership, and control. They enable innovative business models, drive community engagement, and create a new economic landscape.

With applications in various sectors, from finance to arts and governance, tokens are not just a technological phenomenon but a societal shift towards decentralization and democratization. They symbolize a world where value is not confined to physical form or centralized control but is fluid, accessible, and participatory.

By understanding the essence of tokens, we are exploring a fundamental building block of modern digital transformation.

This concludes the subchapter on the definition of tokens. I'll proceed with the next subchapter "1.2 Types of Tokens" in a separate response. Let me know if you have any specific requests or comments on this section!

1.2 Types of Tokens

Tokens have become an integral part of the digital landscape, and understanding their types is crucial for both developers and investors. Each type of token serves a distinct purpose within the ecosystem in which it exists, and different token types offer varying rights, functionalities, and benefits. In this subchapter, we will explore the main types of tokens, namely, Utility Tokens, Security Tokens, and Non-Fungible Tokens (NFTs), along with their characteristics, use cases, and practical examples.

Utility Tokens

Utility tokens, also known as app coins or user tokens, provide users with access to a product or service.

Characteristics:

- **Access to Services**: Utility tokens can be exchanged for services within a specific platform.
- **Incentive Structure**: These tokens often incentivize user engagement and participation within a network.

- **Lack of Ownership Rights**: Utility tokens do not usually confer ownership rights or revenue sharing.

Example: Binance Coin (BNB) can be used to pay for transaction fees on the Binance exchange, allowing users to receive discounts.

Security Tokens

Security tokens are digital representations of ownership in physical or real-world assets, such as real estate, stocks, or bonds.

Characteristics:

- **Asset Backing**: These tokens are often backed by tangible assets, giving intrinsic value.
- **Regulatory Compliance**: Security tokens are typically subject to legal regulations, such as SEC rules in the United States.

- **Ownership and Revenue Rights**: Holders may have rights to dividends, profit sharing, or voting within the organization.

Example: A real estate company may tokenize a commercial property, issuing tokens that represent ownership shares in the building. Token holders could receive rental income proportionate to their holdings.

Non-Fungible Tokens (NFTs)

NFTs are unique digital tokens that cannot be replaced with something else. They are often used to represent ownership of unique digital or physical assets.

Characteristics:

- **Uniqueness**: Each NFT is distinct and represents a specific item or piece of content.

- **Indivisibility**: NFTs usually cannot be divided into smaller parts, unlike cryptocurrencies or other tokens.
- **Proof of Authenticity**: NFTs can provide verifiable proof of ownership and authenticity.

Example: An artist might create a digital painting and issue an NFT that corresponds to it. The holder of the NFT would own the unique digital asset, and the blockchain record would verify its authenticity.

Conclusion

Understanding the types of tokens is fundamental to grasping the diverse applications and opportunities in the digital asset landscape. From the versatile Utility Tokens that enable and incentivize engagement, to the Security Tokens that democratize investment in tangible assets, and the unique Non-Fungible Tokens that redefine ownership of unique assets, the world of tokens is rich and multifaceted.

The categorization of tokens into these primary types is not exhaustive, and the landscape continues to evolve.

Nevertheless, these classifications provide a foundational understanding and a lens through which we can explore the innovative ways in which tokens are reshaping economics, governance, ownership, and interaction in the digital age.

In an era where digital transformation is not merely a technological shift but a redefinition of value, relationships, and systems, tokens stand as symbols of innovation and potential. They bridge the physical and virtual realms, creating new paradigms and opportunities for individuals, organizations, and societies at large.

This concludes the subchapter on types of tokens. Next, we'll explore the historical overview of tokenization in subchapter "1.3 Historical Overview." Let me know if you have any specific requests or comments on this section!

1.3 Historical Overview

The history of tokenization is a rich tapestry that reflects the evolution of digital technology, finance, and societal values. As a transformative concept, tokenization has its roots in the development of cryptocurrencies and has since grown into a multi-dimensional phenomenon encompassing various sectors and applications. In this subchapter, we will explore the historical milestones, the emergence of different token forms, and the impact on the global landscape.

The Dawn of Cryptocurrencies

The genesis of modern tokenization can be traced back to the creation of Bitcoin in 2008 by the pseudonymous Satoshi Nakamoto.

Bitcoin: As the first decentralized cryptocurrency, Bitcoin introduced the idea of digital scarcity and peer-to-peer transactions.

Example: Bitcoin's blockchain allowed users to transfer value without intermediaries, laying the foundation for tokenization concepts.

The Advent of Smart Contracts

The development of smart contracts added a new layer of functionality and complexity to the world of digital assets.

- **Ethereum**: Launched in 2015 by Vitalik Buterin and others, Ethereum introduced the ability to create programmable smart contracts.

Example: The ERC-20 token standard on Ethereum allowed developers to create customizable tokens with specific rules and functions, sparking a wave of innovation in tokenized assets.

Initial Coin Offerings (ICOs)

The concept of ICOs emerged as a novel fundraising mechanism, enabling projects to raise capital through token sales.

Characteristics:

- **Democratic Fundraising**: ICOs democratized investment by allowing anyone to participate.

- **Speculative Nature**: Many ICOs led to speculative investments, resulting in both success stories and significant losses.

Example: Ethereum's own ICO in 2014 raised over $18 million, establishing a precedent for future ICOs.

The Rise of NFTs and DeFi

Recent years have seen the emergence of Non-Fungible Tokens (NFTs) and decentralized finance (DeFi), expanding the scope of tokenization.

- **NFTs**: These tokens represent unique assets, gaining prominence in the art and collectibles space.
- **DeFi**: Tokenization within DeFi has enabled decentralized lending, borrowing, and yield farming.

Example: Platforms like Uniswap use liquidity provider (LP) tokens to represent users' shares in liquidity pools.

Regulatory Landscape

The evolution of tokenization has also led to regulatory scrutiny and development.

- **Regulatory Responses**: Governments and regulators have begun to define legal frameworks to govern tokenized assets.
- **Security Tokens**: The emergence of security tokens as regulated financial instruments has bridged traditional finance and digital assets.

Example: The U.S. Securities and Exchange Commission (SEC) has issued guidelines and rulings on ICOs and security tokens, shaping the legal environment.

Conclusion

The historical overview of tokenization reveals a dynamic and evolving journey that mirrors the broader trends in technology, economics, and society. From the groundbreaking creation of Bitcoin to the sophisticated applications in DeFi, the landscape of tokenization is a testament to human ingenuity and the potential of decentralized systems.

The past, present, and future of tokenization are intertwined with questions of value, ownership, access, and governance. As we continue to explore new frontiers and applications, the history of tokenization serves as both a roadmap and a reflection of our collective aspirations.

Whether in finance, art, real estate, or governance, tokenization stands at the intersection of innovation and transformation, shaping a future where the digital and physical realms coalesce in novel and empowering ways.

This concludes the subchapter on the historical overview of tokenization. Next, we'll proceed with the second part of the book. Let me know if you have any specific requests or comments on this section, or if you'd like to review anything from the previous subchapters!

2. Understanding Asset Tokenization

2.1 Tokenization of Real Assets

Tokenization of real assets is an emerging and transformative process that has the potential to reshape the way we interact with physical assets such as real estate, art, commodities, and even intellectual property. This subchapter will provide an in-depth examination of the concept, the underlying technology, the benefits and challenges, and examples of real-world applications.

Definition and Concept

Tokenization of real assets refers to the process of issuing digital tokens that represent ownership or a claim on physical assets. These tokens can be traded, sold, or held just like traditional securities, but with the added benefits of blockchain technology.

- **Tokenized Ownership**: Each token represents a fractional ownership in the asset, enabling smaller and more accessible investments.

- **Liquidity and Accessibility**: By breaking down high-value assets into smaller units, tokenization can increase liquidity and enable broader participation.

Technology Behind Tokenization

Tokenization relies on blockchain technology and smart contracts to create, manage, and transfer digital tokens.

- **Blockchain**: Provides a decentralized and immutable ledger, ensuring transparency and security.
- **Smart Contracts**: Automates the execution of contractual terms, facilitating transactions and reducing friction.

Example: Real estate properties can be tokenized on Ethereum, with ownership rights, rental income, and other terms programmed into a smart contract.

Benefits of Tokenization

Tokenization offers several benefits that can revolutionize the way we deal with real assets.

Democratization of Investment: Allows smaller investors to participate in markets previously reserved for wealthy individuals or institutions.

- **Increased Liquidity**: Fractional ownership makes buying and selling more flexible, creating a more liquid market.
- **Global Reach**: Tokens can be bought and sold worldwide, breaking down geographical barriers.
- **Transparency and Security**: The use of blockchain ensures that all transactions are transparent, secure, and immutable.

Challenges and Considerations

While promising, tokenization also comes with challenges and considerations that must be addressed.

- **Regulatory Compliance**: Adhering to legal requirements is paramount, especially when dealing with securities and property rights.

- **Interoperability**: Ensuring that different blockchain platforms can interact seamlessly is crucial for broader adoption.
- **Market Adoption**: Building trust and understanding among traditional investors and stakeholders may take time and effort.

Practical Examples

Several real-world applications of tokenization are already in existence, providing insights into its potential.

- **Real Estate**: Platforms like RealT and Mattereum have tokenized properties, allowing investors to buy fractional ownership.
- **Art and Collectibles**: Masterpieces and rare collectibles have been tokenized, enabling broader access to ownership and investment.
- **Commodities**: Tokenization of gold and other precious metals is being explored to create more accessible and transparent markets.

Conclusion

Tokenization of real assets stands as a testament to the innovative application of technology in bridging the physical and digital worlds. By breaking down barriers to entry, enhancing transparency, and creating more fluid markets, tokenization presents a new frontier in investment and ownership.

The journey towards widespread adoption may be filled with challenges and complexities, but the promise of democratizing access, fostering global connections, and redefining value creation makes tokenization of real assets a compelling and transformative avenue to explore.

As we proceed in our exploration of tokenization, the interplay between technology, regulation, human behavior, and societal values will continue to shape the landscape. The potential is vast, and the future is ripe with opportunities.

This concludes the subchapter on tokenization of real assets. Next, we will move on to "2.2 Legal and

Regulatory Framework." If you have any specific requests or comments on this section, please let me know!

2.2 Legal and Regulatory Framework

The tokenization of assets, whether real or digital, necessitates a comprehensive understanding of the legal and regulatory landscape. This subchapter will explore the existing legal frameworks, regulatory compliance requirements, jurisdictional considerations, and the evolving nature of law in the context of tokenization.

Understanding Legal Classifications

Tokenization often involves the creation and distribution of digital tokens that may be classified under various legal categories.

- **Securities Tokens**: Represent ownership in an asset and may fall under securities laws.
- **Utility Tokens**: Provide access to a service or product and may be regulated differently.

Example: The U.S. Securities and Exchange Commission (SEC) may treat tokens sold in an Initial Coin Offering (ICO) as securities, subjecting them to specific legal requirements.

Regulatory Bodies and Jurisdiction

Different countries and regions have their regulatory bodies, and jurisdictional considerations play a vital role.

- **United States**: The SEC, Commodity Futures Trading Commission (CFTC), and Financial Crimes Enforcement Network (FinCEN) are involved in regulating digital assets.
- **European Union**: The European Securities and Markets Authority (ESMA) oversees securities regulations, while individual member states may have specific rules.
- **Asia**: Jurisdictions like Singapore and Hong Kong have established regulatory frameworks for digital assets.

Example: The Monetary Authority of Singapore (MAS) has issued guidelines on digital token offerings, providing clarity on the application of securities laws.

Compliance Requirements

Compliance with legal and regulatory requirements is paramount to the success and legitimacy of tokenization efforts.

- **Anti-Money Laundering (AML) and Know Your Customer (KYC):** Ensuring proper identity verification and monitoring for suspicious activities.
- **Securities Regulations**: Adhering to rules related to the issuance, trading, and management of securities.
- **Consumer Protection**: Ensuring transparency, fairness, and integrity in dealings with consumers.

Example: A tokenized real estate platform must comply with property laws, securities regulations, AML and KYC requirements, and other jurisdiction-specific regulations.

Evolving Legal Landscape

The legal environment surrounding tokenization is dynamic and continues to evolve.

- **Emerging Regulations**: New laws and guidelines are being introduced to address the unique challenges posed by digital assets.
- **Legal Uncertainty**: In some jurisdictions, the lack of clear regulations can create uncertainty and hinder adoption.
- **Cross-Border Considerations**: The global nature of digital assets raises complex legal questions across different jurisdictions.

Example: The European Union's Markets in Crypto-Assets (MiCA) regulation is a recent proposal aimed at harmonizing the treatment of crypto assets across the member states.

Conclusion

The legal and regulatory framework surrounding tokenization is complex, multifaceted, and constantly evolving. Understanding and navigating this landscape is crucial for anyone involved in the creation, distribution, or management of tokenized assets.

From compliance with securities laws to considerations of consumer protection, the intertwining of law and technology creates both challenges and opportunities. Continued dialogue between regulators, legal experts, technologists, and industry stakeholders is essential to shaping a balanced and supportive environment that fosters innovation while safeguarding interests.

As tokenization continues to push boundaries and redefine traditional concepts of ownership, value, and access, the legal and regulatory underpinnings will remain a vital aspect of this transformative journey.

The next subchapter, "2.3 Technical Aspects and Standards," will delve into the technological foundations that make tokenization possible. Please let me know if there's anything specific, you'd like me to cover or if you have any feedback on this section!

2.3 Technical Aspects and Standards

Tokenization is a process that requires the confluence of various technologies, standards, and protocols to function effectively. This subchapter will shed light on the technical dimensions that facilitate the creation, distribution, and management of digital tokens, including blockchain platforms, token standards, security considerations, and interoperability challenges.

Blockchain Platforms

The choice of a blockchain platform is pivotal in determining the characteristics and functionalities of the tokens.

- **Ethereum**: A prominent platform known for its smart contract capabilities, enabling the creation of customizable tokens.
- **Binance Smart Chain**: A platform designed for high-performance applications, providing a scalable environment for token creation.
- **Others**: Platforms like Tezos, Cardano, and Polkadot also offer varying features for tokenization.

Example: ERC-20 is a popular token standard on Ethereum that has been widely adopted for various tokenization projects.

Token Standards

Token standards are predefined rules that govern the creation and interaction of tokens within a blockchain ecosystem.

- **ERC-20**: A widely used standard for fungible tokens, ensuring consistency in how tokens behave within the Ethereum network.

- **ERC-721**: A standard for non-fungible tokens (NFTs), allowing for the creation of unique, indivisible tokens.
- **Other Standards**: Various other standards cater to specific needs and functionalities, such as ERC-1155 for multi-token contracts.

Example: CryptoKitties, a popular game, utilizes the ERC-721 standard to create unique digital cats that can be bought, sold, and bred.

- **Security Considerations**

Security is paramount in tokenization, encompassing various aspects from smart contract auditing to wallet protection.

- **Smart Contract Auditing**: Ensuring that the underlying smart contracts are free from vulnerabilities and errors.
- **Custody Solutions**: Safeguarding the tokens through secure wallet solutions, both hot and cold storage.

- **Multi-Signature Protocols**: Employing multi-signature schemes to add an extra layer of protection.

Example: Many projects opt for third-party auditing firms to rigorously test their smart contracts for potential security flaws.

Interoperability and Integration

Seamless integration between different systems and cross-chain operability is key to broader adoption and functionality.

- **Cross-Chain Protocols**: Enabling tokens to move and interact across different blockchain platforms.
- **API Integration**: Facilitating integration with existing financial systems, exchanges, and other services.
- **Standardization Efforts**: Encouraging the adoption of common standards and protocols to ensure compatibility.

Example: The Polkadot network aims to enable different blockchains to transfer messages and value in a trust-free fashion.

Conclusion

The technical aspects and standards underpinning tokenization provide the foundational architecture that enables the vision of fractional ownership, enhanced liquidity, and democratized access to come to life.

From the choice of the blockchain platform to the careful consideration of security measures, the technical nuances of tokenization offer a multifaceted and complex landscape to navigate. Collaboration between developers, regulators, users, and other stakeholders is essential in shaping an ecosystem that balances innovation, flexibility, security, and compliance.

As technology continues to evolve, so too will the standards and practices governing tokenization. Embracing the complexity and continuously striving for excellence and integrity will ensure that the potential of tokenization is fully realized.

In the next subchapter, "2.4 Market Dynamics and Ecosystem," we will explore the market forces, participants, and the broader ecosystem that contributes to the vibrancy and growth of tokenization. If you have any specific requests or comments on this section, please let me know!

2.4 Market Dynamics and Ecosystem

Tokenization represents not just a technological shift but a transformation in the way value is transferred, accessed, and managed. This subchapter explores the forces shaping the tokenization market, key players in the ecosystem, market trends, opportunities, challenges, and how these factors intertwine to create a thriving environment for digital assets.

- **Market Forces and Trends**

Understanding the key trends and driving forces is essential for anyone participating in or observing the tokenization landscape.

- **Increased Liquidity**: Tokenization often allows assets to be fractionally owned, thereby enhancing liquidity.
- **Democratization of Access**: Tokenized assets can often be accessed by a broader range of investors, reducing entry barriers.
- **Interoperability**: The ability to move tokens across various platforms and blockchains is a growing trend.
- **Regulatory Developments**: An evolving regulatory landscape is both shaping and reacting to the growth of tokenized assets.

Example: The tokenization of art through NFTs has opened the art market to a broader range of investors and enthusiasts.

Key Participants in the Ecosystem

The tokenization ecosystem consists of various players, each contributing to the overall function and growth of the market.

- **Issuers**: Entities or individuals who create and distribute tokens, such as companies tokenizing real estate.
- **Investors**: Both retail and institutional investors who buy and hold tokens.
- **Exchanges**: Platforms where tokens can be traded, bought, and sold.
- **Regulators**: Governing bodies overseeing the legal and compliance aspects.
- **Service Providers**: Entities providing technological solutions, custody, legal advice, etc.

Example: A tokenized real estate project may involve issuers, legal experts, technological partners, exchanges, and investors.

Opportunities

Tokenization offers various opportunities that cater to different market needs and create value in novel ways.

- **Asset Diversification**: Investors can access a wider range of assets, including those previously illiquid or inaccessible.
- **Global Reach**: Tokenized assets can be traded and accessed across borders, reaching a global audience.
- **Innovation in Products and Services**: New products and financial instruments can be created using tokenization.

Example: Tokenized bonds and equities offer innovative ways for companies to raise capital and for investors to gain exposure.

Challenges and Risks

While presenting opportunities, the tokenization landscape is also fraught with challenges and risks.

- **Regulatory Uncertainty**: Ambiguity in regulations can lead to compliance risks.

- **Technical Vulnerabilities**: Security risks in smart contracts or platforms can lead to losses.
- **Market Adoption**: Building trust and understanding among traditional investors and institutions may be a hurdle.

Example: The DAO incident in 2016, where a vulnerability in a smart contract led to significant losses, underscores the importance of security.

Conclusion

The market dynamics and ecosystem surrounding tokenization are rich, complex, and continually evolving. From the innovative ways in which assets are now being represented and traded to the broad spectrum of participants involved, tokenization is reshaping the very fabric of financial interaction.

Understanding the forces at play, the opportunities that beckon, and the challenges that must be navigated is paramount for anyone engaged in this groundbreaking field.

As we transition to the next subchapter, "2.5 Use Cases and Real-World Applications," we will delve into practical examples and explore how tokenization is being applied across various sectors and domains. If you have any feedback or specific areas, you'd like me to cover, please let me know!

2.5 Use Cases and Real-World Applications

Tokenization has moved beyond a novel concept to a pragmatic solution applied across various domains. This subchapter will explore some of the key use cases of tokenization, examining how it's transforming industries such as finance, real estate, art, and more. The insights and examples provided will help illustrate the tangible impact of tokenization.

Financial Instruments

Tokenization of traditional financial products has opened new doors in the financial landscape.

- **Equity Tokenization**: Tokenizing company shares, allowing for fractional ownership and enhanced liquidity.
- **Debt Tokenization**: Bonds and other debt instruments can be tokenized to simplify issuance and trading.
- **Funds and Portfolios**: Tokenized funds enable diversified investment and ease of access.

Example: tZERO, a technology platform, has tokenized equity, allowing investors to trade shares on a regulated platform.

Real Estate

The real estate sector has embraced tokenization to overcome traditional barriers.

- **Fractional Ownership**: Tokenization enables small investors to invest in real estate by purchasing fractions of a property.
- **Streamlined Transactions**: Reduces complexities in buying, selling, and transferring real estate assets.
- **Global Reach**: Tokenized properties can be bought and sold globally, expanding the market.

Example: RealT is a platform that allows investors to buy tokenized shares of real estate properties in the United States.

Art and Collectibles

The world of art and collectibles has been revolutionized by tokenization, particularly through Non-Fungible Tokens (NFTs).

- **Ownership and Provenance**: Tokenization ensures clear ownership and tracks the history of an art piece.

- **Access to Art Market**: NFTs have democratized access to the art market, allowing various artists and collectors to participate.
- **Digital and Physical Art**: Both digital art and physical art can be tokenized, creating new market dynamics.

Example: Beeple's digital artwork sold as an NFT for $69 million, showcasing the potential of tokenized art.

Supply Chain and Authentication

Tokenization offers innovative solutions for supply chain management and product authentication.

- **Tracking and Transparency**: Tokenization allows for transparent tracking of products throughout the supply chain.
- **Authentication**: Tokens can represent genuine products, reducing counterfeiting and fraud.
- **Efficiency and Collaboration**: Enhances coordination among various stakeholders in the supply chain.

Example: De Beers uses tokenization to trace the journey of diamonds from mine to market, ensuring ethical sourcing.

Other Sectors

Tokenization is making inroads into various other sectors, from healthcare to energy.

- **Energy Credits**: Tokenizing energy credits enables transparent and efficient trading.
- **Healthcare Data**: Secure and controlled sharing of healthcare data through tokenization.
- **Intellectual Property**: Tokenizing patents and intellectual property rights.

Example: WePower uses tokenization for trading renewable energy, creating a more accessible and transparent market.

Conclusion

The use cases and real-world applications of tokenization are as varied as they are transformative. From reshaping the financial markets to democratizing the art world, the tangible impact of tokenization is being felt across industries.

The examples provided not only illustrate the breadth and depth of tokenization's reach but also highlight the innovative spirit that drives this technology. The potential applications are vast, and we are only at the cusp of exploring all that tokenization can achieve.

As we move forward to the next subchapter, "2.6 Regulatory and Legal Considerations," we will delve into the complex legal landscape surrounding tokenization, addressing regulatory compliance, jurisdictional challenges, and more. Your insights or specific requests for the upcoming sections are always welcome!

2.6 Regulatory and Legal Considerations

Tokenization, while offering innovation and growth opportunities, also brings forth regulatory challenges and legal intricacies. This subchapter aims to untangle these aspects by addressing the legal frameworks, regulatory compliance, challenges, and evolving legal landscape that governs tokenization.

Legal Frameworks and Classifications

Understanding the legal structure around tokenization is paramount, and it starts with how tokens are classified.

- **Security Tokens**: Governed by securities laws, these tokens represent ownership or a share in an entity or project.
- **Utility Tokens**: Designed to provide access to a specific product or service, often not regulated as securities.
- **Non-Fungible Tokens (NFTs)**: Unique tokens representing a specific asset, with varying legal classifications.

Example: In the U.S., the Howey Test is often used to determine if a token qualifies as a security.

Regulatory Compliance

Compliance with existing regulations is critical for legal operation in the tokenization space.

- **Securities Regulation**: Applicable to tokens classified as securities, requiring compliance with relevant securities laws.
- **Anti-Money Laundering (AML) and Know Your Customer (KYC):** Platforms must adhere to AML and KYC laws to prevent fraud and illegal activities.
- **Tax Compliance**: Tokens may be subject to taxation, requiring understanding and adherence to tax laws.

Example: The SEC's action against Telegram for failing to register its token offering illustrates the importance of securities compliance.

Jurisdictional Challenges

Different jurisdictions have varying regulations, creating complexities for global operations.

- **Diverse Regulatory Landscapes**: Different countries have distinct laws governing tokenization, creating compliance challenges.
- **Cross-Border Operations**: Navigating regulations across various jurisdictions can be complex and requires legal expertise.
- **Global Standardization Efforts**: Initiatives to standardize regulations can mitigate these challenges.

Example: While Switzerland has become a hub for crypto and tokenization, other countries like China have more restrictive regulations.

Evolving Legal Landscape

The legal environment around tokenization is dynamic and continually evolving.

- **New Regulations and Guidance**: Regulators are frequently issuing new rules and guidance, requiring constant vigilance.
- **Legal Precedents**: Court decisions may set precedents that shape the legal landscape.

- **Regulatory Innovation**: Some jurisdictions are creating "regulatory sandboxes" to foster innovation within legal bounds.

Example: The Liechtenstein Blockchain Act is an innovative legal framework specifically designed to govern tokenization.

Ethical and Social Considerations

Tokenization also brings ethical considerations, especially in areas like data privacy and social impact.

- **Data Privacy Compliance**: Tokenization of personal or sensitive data must adhere to privacy laws such as GDPR.
- **Social and Environmental Impact Tokens**: These tokens can drive positive social change but must be handled with care and transparency.

Example: Tokenizing carbon credits to promote sustainability brings ethical considerations in transparency and genuine impact.

Conclusion

The regulatory and legal considerations surrounding tokenization are intricate and vital. From classifications to compliance, jurisdictional challenges to evolving laws, the legal landscape shapes the possibilities and limitations of tokenization.

These considerations underscore the importance of legal expertise, constant monitoring of the evolving landscape, and adherence to ethical standards in the tokenization domain.

As we transition into the next subchapter, "2.7 Risks and Mitigation Strategies," we will explore the various risks associated with tokenization and the strategies to mitigate these risks. As always, your feedback and specific requests are appreciated as we delve deeper into this exciting field!

2.7 Risks and Mitigation Strategies

Tokenization, while holding immense promise, comes with its set of risks and challenges. Identifying these risks, understanding their implications, and crafting mitigation strategies are essential for the successful adoption and implementation of tokenization. This subchapter explores these facets, offering actionable insights.

Technological Risks

The technology that powers tokenization presents risks that must be managed.

- **Smart Contract Vulnerabilities**: Coding errors in smart contracts can lead to exploitation.
- **Cybersecurity Threats**: Threats like hacking can compromise tokens and related systems.
- **Interoperability Issues**: Challenges in interoperating with different blockchains and systems.
- **Mitigation**: Robust code audits, employing security best practices, and ensuring compatibility across platforms.

Example: The DAO hack exploited a smart contract vulnerability, leading to significant losses.

Regulatory and Compliance Risks

Regulatory complexities can pose risks for tokenized projects.

- **Non-Compliance Penalties:** Failure to comply with relevant regulations can result in fines and legal actions.
- **Regulatory Changes**: Sudden changes in regulations can disrupt tokenized initiatives.
- **Mitigation**: Regular legal consultations, ongoing compliance monitoring, and agility in adapting to regulatory changes.

Example: Several Initial Coin Offerings (ICOs) faced legal actions due to non-compliance with securities laws.

Market and Liquidity Risks

Market-related risks are vital considerations in the tokenization landscape.

- **Market Volatility**: Fluctuations in token prices can create instability.

- **Lack of Liquidity**: Limited availability of trading partners may hinder buying/selling of tokens.
- **Mitigation**: Developing a strong market presence, engaging with established exchanges, and transparent communication.

Example: Lack of liquidity in some tokenized real estate assets can make selling properties challenging.

Fraud and Ethical Risks

Ethical considerations and the risk of fraud must be carefully managed.

- **Fraudulent Schemes**: Scams and fraudulent projects can tarnish the reputation of tokenization.
- **Ethical Dilemmas**: Misrepresentation, lack of transparency, and unethical practices can pose risks.
- **Mitigation**: Rigorous due diligence, transparent operations, and adherence to ethical guidelines.

Example: Ponzi schemes involving tokens have led to losses for investors and damaged trust in the ecosystem.

Operational and Strategic Risks

Operational aspects present their unique set of risks and challenges.

- **Operational Failures**: Technical failures, human errors, and other operational issues can disrupt tokenized systems.
- **Strategic Misalignment**: Lack of alignment with business objectives can derail tokenization initiatives.
- **Mitigation**: Implementing robust operational processes, aligning tokenization with strategic goals, and ongoing monitoring.

Example: Poorly executed tokenization strategies have led to the failure of several projects.

Conclusion

Risks in the tokenization landscape are multifaceted, spanning technology, regulation, market, ethics, and operations. Recognizing these risks, understanding their implications, and employing well-thought-out mitigation strategies are fundamental for achieving success in tokenization.

The examples provided shed light on real-world situations, highlighting the importance of a well-balanced approach to risk management.

As we transition into the final subchapter of this section, "2.8 Future Perspectives and Trends," we will look beyond the present, exploring what the future holds for tokenization, the upcoming trends, and the evolving dynamics. Your insights or specific requests for the upcoming sections are always welcome, as we continue to unravel the exciting world of tokenization!

2.8 Future Perspectives and Trends

As the world continues to embrace digital transformation, tokenization is poised to play an increasingly vital role. Understanding the future perspectives and trends in this space not only offers exciting insights but also guides strategic decisions for businesses, regulators, developers, and investors. This subchapter delves into these futuristic vistas.

Emerging Technologies and Innovations

The future of tokenization will likely be shaped by continuous technological innovations.

- **Layer 2 Solutions**: Enhancing scalability and efficiency, such as the Lightning Network on Bitcoin.
- **Interoperable Blockchains**: Allowing seamless communication between different blockchain platforms.
- **Decentralized Finance (DeFi):** Expanding opportunities for financial services through decentralized platforms.

Example: Polkadot's interoperability aims to enable different blockchains to transfer messages and value in a trust-free manner.

New Asset Classes and Applications

Tokenization is likely to expand into new domains and asset classes.

- **Tokenized Intellectual Property**: Enabling creators to tokenize and monetize their intellectual assets.
- **Energy and Environmental Credits**: Tokenizing carbon credits or renewable energy certificates.
- **Virtual and Augmented Reality Assets**: Tokenization of virtual real estate and assets in virtual worlds.

Example: The tokenization of famous artworks has allowed shared ownership and global access.

Regulatory Evolution

The regulatory landscape is anticipated to evolve, striking a balance between innovation and consumer protection.

- **Clearer Regulations:** Defined legal frameworks that provide clarity and certainty.
- **Global Collaboration**: Cross-border regulatory efforts to standardize practices.
- **Emphasis on Consumer Protection**: Ensuring the protection of investors and consumers in tokenized initiatives.

Example: The European Union's Markets in Crypto-Assets (MiCA) regulation aims to provide a comprehensive framework for crypto-assets.

Social and Economic Impact

Tokenization could bring profound social and economic changes.

- **Democratization of Investments**: Providing access to investment opportunities previously reserved for the elite.

- **Social Impact Tokens**: Utilizing tokens to drive positive social changes, like promoting education or healthcare.
- **Economic Inclusion**: Tokenization could foster financial inclusion, especially in underbanked regions.

Example: Tokenized real estate projects that allow small investors to participate in property investments.

Challenges and Potential Roadblocks

Despite the promising trends, future challenges and roadblocks must be recognized.

- **Technology Adoption Barriers**: The complexity and learning curve associated with blockchain technology.
- **Regulatory Uncertainty**: Continued uncertainty in regulations could stifle innovation.
- **Market Resistance**: Skepticism and resistance from traditional market players.

Example: Regulatory crackdowns in certain jurisdictions have posed challenges to crypto and tokenization projects.

Conclusion

The future of tokenization is both exciting and complex, characterized by emerging technologies, new applications, evolving regulations, profound social impacts, and potential challenges. Embracing these future perspectives and trends requires a forward-thinking approach, adaptability, and strategic alignment with the evolving landscape.

As we conclude this section, we prepare to delve into the next part of the book, exploring practical case studies, implementation strategies, and real-world applications of tokenization. Your continued feedback and specific insights for the upcoming chapters are highly appreciated, as we journey further into the dynamic world of tokenizing assets.

3. Business Applications and Case Studies

The potential of tokenization stretches far beyond theoretical discussions and abstract concepts. The real power of this technology comes to life in practical applications, driving tangible benefits for businesses, consumers, and society at large. This chapter uncovers these facets through a detailed examination of business applications, complemented by illustrative case studies.

3.1 Tokenization in Various Industries

Different industries are uniquely poised to benefit from tokenization. This subchapter provides an overview of how tokenization can be applied across various sectors, with insights into specific use cases.

Financial Services

- **Securitization of Assets:** Tokenizing bonds, equities, and other financial instruments.
- **Liquidity Enhancement**: Facilitating trading and market access.

Example: The World Bank's issuance of blockchain-based bonds.

Real Estate

Fractional Ownership: Enabling shared ownership of properties.

- **Streamlining Transactions**: Reducing costs and complexity in real estate deals.

Example: Myco, a platform allowing small investors to invest in premium real estate through tokenization.

Healthcare

Data Sharing and Privacy: Tokenizing healthcare data for secure sharing.

- **Drug Traceability**: Ensuring authenticity and traceability of pharmaceuticals.

Example: Mediledger, using tokenization to create an efficient and secure supply chain for pharmaceuticals.

Entertainment and Arts

- **Monetizing Creativity**: Artists tokenizing their work for broader distribution.
- **Fan Engagement**: Creating unique fan experiences through tokenized rewards.

Example: A famous musician tokenizing an album to enable fan ownership and participation.

Supply Chain and Logistics

- **Traceability and Transparency**: Tokenizing products for end-to-end visibility.
- **Streamlined Operations**: Reducing friction and inefficiencies in supply chains.

Example: De Beers' Tracr, a blockchain platform for tracing the provenance of diamonds.

Sustainability and Environment

- **Green Finance**: Tokenizing green bonds and environmental credits.

- **Sustainable Practices Incentives**: Encouraging eco-friendly practices through token rewards.

Example: A platform that tokenizes carbon credits to encourage companies to reduce emissions.

Conclusion

Tokenization is reshaping industries, creating opportunities for innovation, inclusiveness, efficiency, and sustainability. By examining the above examples, it's evident that the application of tokenization is diverse, bridging gaps and breaking down barriers.

As we prepare to delve into more specific strategies, models, and frameworks in the upcoming subchapters, your insights, questions, or specific areas of interest will be valuable in tailoring the content to your needs.

The exploration of tokenization in the business world is just beginning, and the forthcoming sections will unfold more layers of understanding and practical wisdom. Stay engaged as we delve further into this fascinating journey!

3.2 Strategies and Methodologies for Tokenization

Implementing tokenization requires strategic thinking, careful planning, adherence to best practices, and understanding the potential challenges. This subchapter provides a roadmap for businesses and organizations to successfully implement tokenization.

Planning and Feasibility Study

Starting any tokenization initiative requires thorough planning and a feasibility study.

- **Identifying Opportunities**: Understanding where tokenization can add value.
- **Assessing Risks**: Evaluating the regulatory, technical, and market risks.
- **Resource Allocation**: Determining the budget, technology, and human resources needed.

Example: A real estate company conducts a feasibility study to evaluate the tokenization of a commercial property, assessing legal compliance, market interest, and technical requirements.

Choosing the Right Technology and Platform

Selecting the correct technology and platform is pivotal to the success of the tokenization process.

- **Blockchain Selection**: Whether to use a public, private, or consortium blockchain.
- **Smart Contract Development**: Creating secure and efficient smart contracts to govern the tokens.
- **Interoperability Considerations**: Ensuring that the chosen technology can interact with other systems.

Example: A financial institution opts for Ethereum due to its robust smart contract functionality when tokenizing bonds.

Compliance and Regulatory Considerations

Compliance with laws and regulations is paramount in tokenization.

- **Understanding Legal Requirements**: Engaging with legal experts to understand jurisdiction-specific regulations.
- **Data Privacy Considerations**: Ensuring that tokenization aligns with data protection laws.
- **Licensing and Permissions**: Acquiring necessary licenses or approvals from regulatory authorities.

Example: A startup planning to tokenize art collections consults with legal experts to comply with securities laws and intellectual property rights.

Designing the Token Economy

Creating an efficient token economy involves defining the token's functionalities, distribution, and governance.

- **Token Type Definition**: Deciding whether the token represents equity, debt, utility, etc.
- **Distribution Mechanism**: Planning how tokens will be issued, sold, or distributed.

- **Token Governance**: Establishing rules for voting, decision-making, and updates.

Example: A renewable energy company designs a token economy to incentivize green practices among consumers, defining the token's utility, distribution through rewards, and participatory governance.

Security Considerations

Ensuring robust security measures is crucial to safeguarding the integrity of the tokenization process.

- **Smart Contract Audits**: Conducting thorough audits to prevent vulnerabilities.
- **Data Security Measures**: Implementing encryption, access controls, and secure storage solutions.
- **Ongoing Monitoring**: Regularly monitoring and updating security protocols.

Example: A company tokenizing its shares implements multi-signature wallets, conducts third-party security audits, and establishes ongoing security monitoring.

Community Engagement and Marketing

Building a community and marketing the token effectively can foster success.

- **Transparency and Communication**: Engaging the community with regular updates.
- **Marketing Strategies**: Utilizing various channels to promote the token to the target audience.
- **Feedback Mechanisms**: Creating channels for community feedback and participation.

Example: A game developer tokenizing in-game assets leverages social media and community forums to promote the tokens and gather feedback.

Conclusion

Successfully implementing tokenization demands a holistic approach encompassing planning, technological selection, compliance, token economy design, security, and community engagement. Adhering to this strategic roadmap can help businesses unlock the transformative potential of tokenization, tailoring solutions to their unique context and objectives.

3.3 Challenges, Risks, and Ethical Considerations

Tokenization, though promising, is not devoid of challenges, risks, and ethical questions. This subchapter aims to provide an understanding of these facets, coupled with solutions and mitigation strategies.

Technological Challenges

The complexities of the underlying technology can present numerous challenges.

- **Interoperability Issues**: The compatibility of different blockchain systems and legacy systems.
- **Scalability Concerns**: Managing high transaction volumes without performance degradation.

- **Security Vulnerabilities**: Ensuring robust security against potential attacks and flaws.

Example: A company faces scalability issues with its tokenized loyalty program and opts to use a Layer 2 solution to enhance transaction speed and efficiency.

Regulatory and Compliance Risks

Legal and regulatory aspects pose significant challenges in different jurisdictions.

- **Regulatory Uncertainty**: Lack of clear regulatory guidelines in some regions.
- **Compliance Complexity**: Ensuring adherence to a multitude of local and international laws.
- **Licensing Challenges**: Obtaining necessary licenses and approvals, especially in highly regulated sectors.

Example: A startup tokenizing agricultural land must navigate complex land ownership laws, environmental regulations, and financial compliance requirements.

Market and Financial Risks

Understanding and managing market-related risks is crucial for the success of any tokenization project.

- **Market Adoption Risk**: Challenges related to market acceptance and adoption of tokenized assets.
- **Price Volatility**: The instability of token prices, especially if connected to cryptocurrencies.
- **Liquidity Constraints**: Ensuring sufficient liquidity for token trading.

Example: An energy firm's tokenized green bonds face market adoption challenges due to investor unfamiliarity with tokenized assets, requiring intensive education and marketing efforts.

Ethical Considerations and Social Impact

The ethical implications of tokenization can have far-reaching consequences on society.

- **Data Privacy and Consent**: Ensuring proper handling of personal data and informed consent.
- **Inequality and Accessibility**: Addressing potential disparities in access to tokenized services.
- **Environmental Impact**: Considering the energy consumption of blockchain technologies.

Example: An educational platform tokenizes student data, sparking debates on ethical usage, consent, and potential biases in access to educational resources.

Mitigation Strategies

Understanding challenges and risks allows for the development of mitigation strategies.

- **Due Diligence and Risk Assessment**: Regularly evaluating and updating risk profiles.
- **Legal Consultation and Compliance Monitoring**: Engaging legal experts and ensuring ongoing compliance.

- **Technological Best Practices**: Implementing robust technologies and security measures.

Community and Stakeholder Engagement: Encouraging transparency, participation, and feedback.

Example: A healthcare provider implementing tokenized patient records employs robust security measures, legal consultations, ongoing compliance checks, and engages patients through transparency and feedback channels.

Conclusion

Tokenization's landscape is complex and requires a nuanced understanding of the challenges, risks, and ethical considerations. By acknowledging these aspects and implementing thoughtful mitigation strategies, businesses can navigate the complex terrain and harness tokenization's full potential.

3.4 Real-World Applications and Case Studies

The transformative power of tokenization extends across various domains, sectors, and industries. This subchapter explores real-world applications and case studies, illustrating how tokenization is not merely a theoretical concept but a practical tool driving innovation.

Real Estate Tokenization

Tokenizing property and real estate offer a new paradigm of investment and ownership.

- **Fractional Ownership**: Enabling smaller investors to own fractions of a property.
- **Increased Liquidity**: Making real estate trading more fluid and accessible.

Example: A commercial building is tokenized, allowing individuals to invest as little as $100. This attracts a wider range of investors, democratizing real estate investment.

Tokenization in Finance and Banking

The financial industry is experiencing a significant shift due to tokenization.

- **Tokenized Bonds and Stocks**: Making trading and ownership more efficient.
- **Enhanced Compliance and Transparency**: Leveraging blockchain's transparent and immutable nature.

Example: A global bank tokenizes corporate bonds, enhancing the efficiency of trading and settlement processes, and providing real-time compliance checks.

Art and Cultural Asset Tokenization

Tokenization offers new opportunities in the art and cultural domain.

- **Democratizing Art Ownership**: Enabling fractional ownership of artworks.

- **Provenance and Authenticity Tracking**: Ensuring authenticity through blockchain.

Example: A famous painting is tokenized, allowing art enthusiasts to invest in fractional shares. The blockchain record ensures provenance and authenticity.

Energy and Environmental Tokenization

Tokenization can promote sustainability and environmental stewardship.

- **Green Energy Credits**: Tokenizing renewable energy credits and incentives.
- **Carbon Credit Trading**: Facilitating efficient trading of carbon offset credits.

Example: A renewable energy company tokenizes solar energy credits, incentivizing green energy production and consumption.

Tokenization in Healthcare

Healthcare can benefit from tokenization in unique ways.

- **Patient Data Management**: Secure and efficient handling of patient records.
- **Drug Traceability**: Ensuring authenticity and compliance in the pharmaceutical supply chain.

Example: A hospital network tokenizes patient data, ensuring secure access and streamlined data sharing across medical professionals.

Tokenization in Education

Tokenization offers new perspectives in education and academia.

- **Credential Verification**: Simplifying the verification of educational credentials.
- **Resource Sharing**: Enabling shared access to educational resources.

Example: A university tokenizes diplomas and certificates, ensuring quick and indisputable verification by employers and institutions.

Challenges and Lessons Learned

Examining real-world applications also reveals challenges and valuable lessons.

- **Regulatory Hurdles**: Navigating complex and evolving legal landscapes.
- **Technical Complexities**: Managing technological challenges and integration.
- **Stakeholder Engagement**: Ensuring buy-in from various stakeholders.

Example: A startup facing regulatory challenges in tokenizing agricultural assets learns to work closely with regulators and engage local communities for successful implementation.

Conclusion

Exploring real-world applications and case studies has given us a tangible view of how tokenization is shaping industries, solving problems, and offering new opportunities. From finance to healthcare, art to energy, the potential of tokenization is being realized across diverse landscapes.

3.5 Future Prospects, Emerging Trends, and Innovation

Tokenization has already made significant strides, but its journey is far from over. This subchapter aims to shine a light on what the future might hold, outlining the emerging trends, anticipated innovations, and how these aspects could revolutionize various domains.

Future Prospects in Different Sectors

Understanding how tokenization might evolve in various sectors provides a roadmap for what to expect.

- **Real Estate:** Further democratization, new investment models, and integration with smart contracts.
- **Finance**: Expansion into various financial instruments, improved regulatory compliance tools.
- **Healthcare**: Advanced security for patient data, tokenized medical research.
- **Education**: Widespread use of tokenized credentials, personalized learning paths.

Example: A future where tokenized patient data in healthcare enables personalized medical treatments based on AI-analyzed tokenized health histories.

Technological Innovations

New technologies will drive the next wave of innovation in tokenization.

- **Layer 2 Solutions:** Enhancing scalability and performance.
- **Quantum-Resistant Cryptography:** Preparing for potential quantum computing threats.
- **Integration with IoT:** Tokenizing physical assets and automating processes.

Example: A smart city integrates IoT with tokenized assets, enabling automated toll collection, energy distribution, and more, all governed by transparent tokenized agreements.

Emerging Business Models

Tokenization will likely foster entirely new business models and strategies.

- **Decentralized Finance (DeFi):** Pioneering new ways to interact with financial systems.
- **Collaborative Ownership Models**: Enabling shared ownership and governance of businesses.
- **Subscription and Access Models:** Tokenized access to services and products.

Example: A decentralized autonomous organization (DAO) forms around tokenized community assets, where token holders vote on decisions, collectively managing and benefiting from shared resources.

Social and Environmental Impact

Tokenization has the potential to contribute positively to societal and environmental goals.

- **Environmental Stewardship**: Promoting green initiatives through tokenized incentives.
- **Community Empowerment**: Leveraging tokenization for community-driven projects.
- **Accessibility and Inclusion**: Reducing barriers to entry in various sectors.

Example: A local community tokenizes a shared urban garden, enabling inclusive participation, decision-making, and distribution of produce.

Challenges and Risk Factors

While the future looks promising, it is also filled with uncertainties and challenges.

- **Regulatory Evolution**: Keeping up with changing and inconsistent regulations.
- **Technological Risks**: Managing technological advancements and potential flaws.
- **Market Adoption:** Overcoming skepticism and resistance to new tokenized models.

Example: A company pioneering tokenized insurance products faces challenges in regulatory alignment, technological integration, and market education.

Conclusion

The future of tokenization is a thrilling frontier, laden with opportunities, innovations, and uncertainties. The trends we see emerging today are seeds that could blossom into integral aspects of tomorrow's economic and social fabric.

4. Tokenizing Real Estate

4.1 International and National Regulatory Frameworks

Tokenization, being a technology that leverages blockchain and cryptographic principles, inherently interacts with legal domains ranging from financial regulations to data protection. This subchapter will provide an insightful view into the international and national regulatory frameworks that govern tokenization.

International Regulatory Overview

The international regulatory landscape presents both opportunities and challenges for tokenization.

- **Global Standards and Guidelines**: Overview of international bodies setting standards, such as the Financial Action Task Force (FATF).
- **Cross-Border Collaboration**: Examining agreements and collaborations between different jurisdictions.

Example: The European Union's Markets in Crypto-Assets (MiCA) regulation that aims to provide a harmonized framework for crypto assets across EU member states.

National Regulatory Landscapes

Different countries have unique approaches to regulating tokenization. Some notable examples include:

- **United States**: Exploring the SEC's stance on tokenized securities and the Commodity Futures Trading Commission's (CFTC) view on commodities.
- **European Union**: Assessing the regulatory environment in major European countries, like Germany's BaFin and France's AMF.
- **Asian Markets**: Understanding regulatory developments in countries like Singapore, Japan, and South Korea.

Example: South Korea's Special Financial Information Law (SFIL) and its impact on crypto businesses and tokenization.

Regulatory Challenges and Complexities

The intersection of technology and law presents unique challenges and complexities.

- **Jurisdictional Conflicts**: Handling differences and conflicts between various legal jurisdictions.
- **Innovation vs. Regulation Dilemma**: Balancing the drive for innovation with the need for consumer protection and regulatory compliance.

Example: A tokenized real estate platform navigating the differing real estate laws in multiple jurisdictions, requiring localized legal expertise and compliance measures.

Emerging Regulatory Trends

As tokenization evolves, regulatory landscapes adapt and present new trends.

- **Regulatory Sandboxes**: Providing a controlled environment for innovation and experimentation.

Consumer Protection Initiatives: Enhancing measures to protect participants in tokenized platforms.

- **Regulation of Decentralized Finance (DeFi)**: Understanding how decentralized systems are becoming subjects of regulatory scrutiny.

Example: The UK's Financial Conduct Authority (FCA) using a regulatory sandbox to facilitate innovative fintech projects, including those related to tokenization.

The Role of Self-Regulation and Industry Standards

The tokenization industry is also contributing to its regulatory framework.

- **Industry-Led Initiatives**: Exploring self-regulatory organizations (SROs) and industry-led standards.
- **Best Practices and Ethical Guidelines**: Assessing how industry players are creating self-governance models.

Example: The Global Digital Finance (GDF) and its code of conduct guiding crypto asset companies and platforms.

Conclusion

The legal and regulatory landscape for tokenization is complex and multifaceted, reflecting the innovative nature of the technology itself. Understanding this landscape is essential for anyone looking to participate in or leverage tokenization.

While filled with challenges and intricacies, the regulatory world also offers pathways for collaboration, innovation, and growth. The interplay between international and national laws, emerging trends, and industry-led initiatives paints a vivid picture of a field in constant evolution.

4.2 Legal Considerations and Case Law

Tokenization's innovative nature presents intriguing legal considerations. As it disrupts traditional models, it engages with existing laws, sometimes harmoniously and other times contentiously. Understanding these legal considerations and learning from actual cases can offer valuable insights.

Token Classification and Its Legal Implications

How tokens are classified legally can have substantial consequences.

- **Security Tokens**: Legal obligations under securities laws, registration requirements.
- **Utility Tokens**: Regulatory implications, consumer protection considerations.
- **Payment Tokens**: Compliance with anti-money laundering (AML) and other financial regulations.

Example: The U.S. SEC's case against Telegram, focusing on whether the tokens sold in its ICO were securities under U.S. law.

Intellectual Property (IP) Rights

Tokenization and IP interact in complex ways, impacting creators, owners, and consumers.

- **Tokenizing IP Rights**: Leveraging blockchain for proof of ownership, licensing.
- **Protecting IP in Tokenized Systems**: Legal tools, rights enforcement.

Example: Myco, a fictional company, uses tokenization to represent ownership of patents, allowing fractional ownership and trading of IP rights.

Privacy and Data Protection

Tokenization must comply with existing privacy and data protection laws.

- **General Data Protection Regulation (GDPR):** How tokenization interacts with EU's stringent privacy laws.
- **Handling Personal Data:** Considerations in designing tokenized systems to comply with global privacy standards.

Example: Tokenizing personal data in a healthcare system, ensuring compliance with HIPAA in the U.S.

Consumer Protection and Liability

Consumers' rights and potential liabilities must be considered in tokenized systems.

- **Disclosure Requirements:** Providing consumers with the necessary information and transparency.
- **Dispute Resolution:** Legal mechanisms for resolving conflicts in tokenized transactions.

Example: A tokenized real estate investment platform provides transparent disclosures and incorporates an arbitration clause for dispute resolution.

Case Law: A Deeper Dive

Exploring actual cases provides tangible insights into how laws are applied to tokenization.

- **SEC v. Kik Interactive**: Analyzing how the SEC applied securities laws to Kik's token sale.
- **The DAO Hack**: Investigating legal responses to a hack in a tokenized, decentralized autonomous organization.

Example: Analyzing the legal implications and response to the Mt. Gox exchange hack, involving stolen Bitcoin.

Conclusion

Tokenization's legal landscape is a mosaic of interrelated considerations, ranging from token classification to intellectual property rights, privacy, consumer protection, and specific case law. Understanding these aspects is pivotal for anyone engaging with tokenized assets, whether as an entrepreneur, investor, regulator, or legal professional.

4.3 Token Creation, Deployment, and Management

The creation, deployment, and management of tokens encompass a multitude of elements. This subchapter focuses on the technical aspects, as well as the strategic considerations that must be evaluated during these processes. We'll also provide practical examples to help illuminate these complex topics.

Token Creation: Methods and Considerations

Token creation is the process of developing a digital representation of value or rights. Several factors need to be considered:

- **Token Standards**: Understanding prevalent standards like ERC-20, ERC-721.
- **Smart Contracts**: Utilizing programmable contracts to define token behavior.
- **Use Cases and Design Considerations**: Tailoring the token to specific applications, like digital art, real estate, or supply chain management.

Example: CryptoKitties using ERC-721 standard for unique, non-fungible tokens representing virtual cats.

- **Deployment**: Launching Tokens into the Market

Deploying tokens involves several critical steps and considerations:

Initial Coin Offerings (ICOs) or Token Sales: Structuring the launch, legal compliance, marketing.

- **Exchanges and Trading Platforms**: Listing tokens on various platforms for trading.
- **Security and Auditing**: Ensuring robust security measures, engaging third-party audits.

Example: The successful launch of Chainlink's LINK token through an ICO, followed by listings on major exchanges.

Token Management: Operations and Governance

Ongoing management of tokens requires focus on:

- **Lifecycle Management**: Overseeing the entire lifecycle of tokens, from issuance to redemption or destruction.
- **Governance Models**: Implementing mechanisms for decision-making, updates, and community involvement.
- **Compliance and Reporting**: Adhering to regulatory requirements, providing transparency.

Example: MakerDAO's governance model allowing token holders to vote on critical parameters of the decentralized finance system.

Technical Considerations and Infrastructure

A comprehensive understanding of underlying technology is crucial:

- **Blockchain Selection**: Choosing the right blockchain platform, such as Ethereum, Binance Smart Chain, or a custom-built solution.

- **Interoperability**: Enabling interaction with other tokens, blockchains, or traditional systems.
- **Scalability and Performance**: Ensuring the system can handle the required volume and speed.

Example: The Tether (USDT) stablecoin, deployed across multiple blockchains for increased interoperability and efficiency.

Risk Management and Security

Robust risk management practices must be integrated:

- **Security Protocols**: Employing state-of-the-art security measures to protect against breaches and attacks.
- **Risk Assessment**: Regularly evaluating and mitigating various risks, including legal, financial, and operational.
- **Disaster Recovery Plans**: Establishing processes for recovering from unexpected events or failures.

Example: A tokenized investment fund implementing multifactor authentication, cold storage, and regular security audits.

Conclusion

Token creation, deployment, and management encompass a sophisticated blend of technical prowess, strategic planning, regulatory compliance, and risk management. The journey from conceptualizing a token to sustaining its operation in the market is multifaceted and requires careful consideration of numerous factors.

4.4 Tokenization in Different Sectors and Industries

Tokenization is a versatile technology with applications that stretch across various sectors and industries. This subchapter will focus on exploring how tokenization is being applied, highlighting specific examples, and illustrating the benefits and challenges within each area.

Financial Services and Banking

The financial sector has been at the forefront of embracing tokenization.

- **Tokenized Securities**: Streamlining the trading, clearing, and settlement of securities.
- **Stablecoins**: Digital tokens pegged to fiat currencies, enhancing speed and reducing costs.
- **Liquidity and Access**: Enabling fractional ownership and expanding investment opportunities.

Example: JP Morgan Chase's launch of the JPM Coin, a digital token to facilitate instant payment transfers.

Real Estate

Tokenization is transforming the real estate industry by unlocking new possibilities.

- **Fractional Ownership**: Allowing multiple investors to own shares in a property.
- **Liquidity and Transparency**: Simplifying transactions and providing real-time data.

- **Cross-Border Investments**: Facilitating international investments in real estate.

Example: Myco Properties, a fictional real estate company, uses tokenization to offer fractional ownership of commercial buildings, lowering the entry barriers for investors.

Supply Chain and Logistics

Tokenization enhances transparency and efficiency within the supply chain.

- **Tracking and Authentication**: Real-time tracking of products, anti-counterfeiting measures.
- **Smart Contracts**: Automating contracts and payments, reducing delays.
- **Sustainability**: Promoting ethical sourcing and environmental responsibility.

Example: De Beers' Tracr platform uses tokenization to track the journey of diamonds from the mine to the consumer, ensuring authenticity and ethical sourcing.

Art and Collectibles

Tokenization is revolutionizing the way we interact with art and collectibles.

- **Provenance and Authenticity**: Verifying the authenticity and ownership history.
- **Access and Democratization**: Enabling fractional ownership of high-value artworks.
- **Digital Art and NFTs**: Empowering digital artists through non-fungible tokens.

Example: Beeple's sale of a digital artwork as an NFT for $69 million, altering the dynamics of the art market.

Healthcare

Tokenization has promising applications within the healthcare sector.

- **Data Sharing and Privacy**: Facilitating secure and controlled sharing of medical data.
- **Personalized Medicine**: Enabling patient-centric approaches through tokenized data.

- **Clinical Trials**: Streamlining processes and enhancing collaboration.

Example: A fictional healthcare provider utilizing tokenization to allow patients to control access to their medical records, enhancing privacy, and facilitating research.

Energy and Utilities

Tokenization is finding innovative applications within energy and utilities.

- **Green Energy Credits**: Tokenizing renewable energy certificates and incentives.
- **Grid Management**: Enabling decentralized and efficient energy distribution.
- **Sustainable Practices**: Encouraging environmentally friendly energy production.

Example: The Brooklyn Microgrid project, using tokenization to enable a community-driven, decentralized energy grid.

Conclusion

The applications of tokenization across various sectors and industries are both transformative and diverse. From redefining investment in real estate to enhancing transparency in the supply chain, the integration of tokenization is reshaping traditional paradigms.

4.5 Legal and Regulatory Compliance in Tokenization

As tokenization finds increasing applications across various sectors, the legal and regulatory environment is becoming increasingly important. This subchapter aims to provide an in-depth understanding of the complexities, challenges, and strategies for ensuring compliance within the ever-evolving legal landscape.

Introduction to Legal Considerations

Understanding the legal aspects is pivotal for any tokenization project.

- **Jurisdictional Differences**: Legal requirements differ across jurisdictions, necessitating careful consideration.
- **Regulatory Classification**: Understanding whether the token is classified as a security, utility, or other type under applicable laws.
- **Compliance Requirements**: Adhering to relevant laws and regulations, such as KYC (Know Your Customer) and AML (Anti-Money Laundering) rules.

Example: Telegram's halted TON project, faced legal challenges with the SEC, highlighting the importance of legal compliance.

Regulatory Agencies and Frameworks

Several regulatory agencies govern the use of tokens.

- **Securities and Exchange Commission (SEC):** Oversees tokens classified as securities in the U.S.

- **Commodity Futures Trading Commission (CFTC):** Regulates commodity and derivatives markets.
- **European Securities and Markets Authority (ESMA):** Governs financial markets in the European Union.

Example: The SEC's enforcement action against Ripple's XRP token, illustrating the agency's regulatory power.

Legal Challenges and Risks

Navigating the legal landscape can be fraught with challenges.

- **Regulatory Uncertainty**: Rapidly changing and often unclear regulations.
- **Cross-Border Complexities**: Conflicting laws and regulations across different countries.
- **Litigation Risks**: Potential legal disputes and enforcement actions.

Example: Bitfinex's legal battle in the context of the issuance of Tether (USDT), showcasing litigation risks.

Best Practices for Legal Compliance

Adopting best practices is essential to mitigate risks and ensure compliance.

- **Legal Consultation**: Engaging with experienced legal professionals with expertise in tokenization.
- **Comprehensive Documentation**: Maintaining detailed records of all activities, decisions, and compliance efforts.
- **Regular Monitoring and Updating**: Staying abreast of legal developments and adjusting strategies accordingly.

Example: Ethereum's careful structuring of its initial offering to comply with legal requirements, serving as a model for others.

Ethical Considerations and Social Responsibility

Compliance also extends to ethical behavior and social responsibility.

- **Transparency and Integrity**: Upholding transparency in operations and dealing with stakeholders with integrity.
- **Social Impact and Responsibility**: Aligning tokenization efforts with broader societal goals and responsible practices.
- **Consumer Protection**: Ensuring robust measures to protect consumers and their data.

Example: Fair Trade Coffee Chain using tokenization to ensure ethical sourcing and fair payment, demonstrating alignment with social responsibility.

Conclusion

Legal and regulatory compliance in tokenization is a multifaceted and critical aspect that requires diligent attention and expertise. The dynamic nature of laws, varying jurisdictional requirements, and the novel characteristics of tokens present unique challenges that must be navigated with precision and care.

4.6 Tokenization Technology: Platforms, Protocols, and Mechanisms

Tokenization technology is the backbone of digital asset representation, and understanding its intricacies is crucial for anyone venturing into the space. This subchapter will guide you through the platforms, protocols, and mechanisms that underpin tokenization, providing insights and examples along the way.

Tokenization Platforms

Various platforms enable the creation, issuance, and management of tokens.

- **Ethereum**: The most widely used platform for creating and managing tokens, especially ERC-20 and ERC-721 standards.
- **Binance Smart Chain**: Known for its efficiency and compatibility with Ethereum.

- **Tezos**: Emphasizing formal verification and security.

Example: CryptoKitties, a popular NFT game, runs on the Ethereum platform.

Token Standards

Token standards provide the rules and guidelines for creating tokens.

- **ERC-20**: The standard for fungible tokens, used in many ICOs and DeFi projects.
- **ERC-721:** For non-fungible tokens (NFTs), each with unique characteristics.
- **ERC-1400:** A security token standard providing additional features for regulatory compliance.

Example: The famous decentralized exchange Uniswap utilizes ERC-20 tokens for trading pairs.

Security and Encryption Mechanisms

Security is paramount in tokenization technology.

- **Public and Private Keys**: The cornerstone of cryptographic security, enabling secure transactions.
- **Multi-Signature Wallets**: Requiring multiple parties to authorize a transaction, enhancing security.
- **Hardware Wallets**: Storing private keys offline to minimize hacking risks.

Example: BitGo's multi-signature wallet solution offers enhanced security for token storage and management.

Interoperability and Cross-Chain Solutions

Interoperability allows tokens to interact across different blockchain platforms.

- **Polkadot**: Facilitating communication and value transfer between distinct blockchains.
- **Cosmos**: Known as the "Internet of Blockchains," enabling interoperability.
- **Atomic Swaps**: Allowing direct, peer-to-peer exchanges between different tokens.

Example: ThorChain's decentralized liquidity network facilitates cross-chain swaps without relying on centralized parties.

Decentralized Finance (DeFi) and Tokenization

DeFi leverages tokenization to create decentralized financial products and services.

- **Liquidity Pools**: Enabling decentralized trading and providing liquidity.
- **Lending and Borrowing**: Using tokens as collateral for decentralized loans.
- **Yield Farming**: Earning rewards through various DeFi protocols.

Example: Compound, a decentralized lending platform, allows users to borrow and lend tokens.

Challenges and Future Directions

Tokenization technology also faces challenges and is constantly evolving.

- **Scalability Issues**: Handling increased transaction volumes while maintaining efficiency.
- **Regulatory Alignment**: Ensuring that technology meets evolving legal requirements.
- **Sustainability Considerations**: Minimizing the environmental impact of blockchain operations.

Example: Ethereum's transition to ETH 2.0, aiming to address scalability and sustainability.

Conclusion

Tokenization technology is a fascinating and complex field, encompassing diverse platforms, protocols, and mechanisms that enable the digital representation of assets. From the standards guiding token creation to the cutting-edge solutions for interoperability, this subchapter has delved into the key components that shape the technology of tokenization.

4.7 Market Dynamics, Trends, and Strategies in Tokenization

The market for tokenized assets is vibrant, complex, and evolving. From emerging trends to key strategies for success, this subchapter explores the multifaceted dynamics of the tokenization market, offering insights, examples, and guidance for navigating this exciting field.

Understanding Market Dynamics

Market dynamics encompass the various factors influencing the demand, supply, pricing, and growth of tokenized assets.

- **Demand Factors**: Driven by investor interest, technological adoption, regulatory clarity, etc.
- **Supply Factors**: Related to the issuance of new tokens, asset types, platform availability, etc.
- **Price Mechanisms**: Influenced by liquidity, trading volumes, speculative behavior, and market sentiment.

Example: The 2017 ICO boom driven by high demand and speculative investments, leading to significant market dynamics shifts.

Key Market Trends

Identifying and understanding the latest trends is vital for positioning within the market.

- **DeFi Growth**: Decentralized Finance is expanding, with tokens playing a central role.
- **NFT Popularity**: Non-fungible tokens (NFTs) capturing mainstream interest in art, collectibles, etc.
- **Security Token Offerings (STOs):** A regulated alternative to ICOs, growing in adoption.
- **Sustainable and Social Impact Tokens**: Focus on environmental and social causes.

Example: Beeple's NFT sale at Christie's for $69 million, signifying the growing trend of high-profile NFTs.

Market Participants and Roles

Understanding the different players in the market and their roles can inform strategic positioning.

- **Issuers**: Entities issuing tokens, such as startups, corporations, or artists.
- **Investors**: Individuals or institutional investors acquiring tokens for various purposes.
- **Exchanges and Trading Platforms**: Facilitating the buying and selling of tokens.
- **Regulators and Governing Bodies**: Overseeing compliance and setting legal standards.

Example: Coinbase, as a leading cryptocurrency exchange, playing a critical role in providing access to token markets.

Market Analysis and Strategy Development

Comprehensive market analysis leads to the formulation of effective strategies.

- **SWOT Analysis**: Analyzing Strengths, Weaknesses, Opportunities, and Threats.

- **Competitive Landscape**: Understanding competitors, market positioning, and differentiation.
- **Regulatory Compliance Strategy**: Ensuring alignment with legal requirements.
- **Technology and Security Considerations**: Assessing technological needs and security measures.

Example: Binance's expansion strategy, utilizing regulatory compliance and technological innovation to extend its market reach.

Challenges and Risks in Market Dynamics

Navigating the market also involves recognizing potential challenges and risks.

- **Regulatory Changes**: Unexpected shifts in legal landscapes.
- **Market Volatility**: Price fluctuations and unpredictable market behavior.
- **Competition and Innovation Risks**: Staying ahead in a rapidly evolving market.

Example: The regulatory crackdown on various cryptocurrency projects, causing market instability and challenges.

Conclusion

The market dynamics, trends, and strategies in tokenization form a complex and exciting panorama. From the underlying forces that drive market behavior to the cutting-edge trends shaping the future, this subchapter has provided a robust exploration of the multifaceted world of tokenized assets.

With illustrative examples and strategic insights, we have ventured into the heart of the tokenization market, uncovering the keys to success, the pitfalls to avoid, and the vision to embrace.

4.8 Legal and Regulatory Considerations in Tokenization

Tokenization is not just a technological marvel but also a subject of extensive legal and regulatory scrutiny. This subchapter dives into the legal frameworks, compliance requirements, and regulatory considerations that govern the creation, issuance, trading, and management of tokenized assets. It highlights the complex interplay between law, technology, and business in the rapidly evolving field of tokenization.

Legal Classification of Tokens

Different jurisdictions classify tokens in various ways, leading to diverse legal implications.

- **Utility Tokens**: Provide access to a product or service and are typically not considered securities.
- **Security Tokens**: Represent ownership or economic rights and are subject to securities laws.
- **Non-Fungible Tokens (NFTs)**: Have unique legal considerations due to their individual characteristics.

Example: The U.S. SEC's regulation of certain ICOs as securities offerings, based on the characteristics of the tokens involved.

Regulatory Compliance for Issuers

Issuers of tokens must adhere to specific regulatory guidelines and compliance measures.

- **Know Your Customer (KYC) and Anti-Money Laundering (AML) Laws**: Verification of customers' identities to prevent illicit activities.
- **Securities Regulations**: Compliance with securities laws for security tokens.
- **Consumer Protection Laws**: Ensuring fairness and transparency in token offerings.

Example: The issuance of security tokens via Security Token Offerings (STOs) requires adherence to specific SEC regulations in the U.S.

Regulation of Exchanges and Trading Platforms

Trading platforms dealing with tokens are subject to various regulatory requirements.

- **Licensing and Registration**: Obtaining the necessary licenses to operate legally.

- **Trading and Reporting Obligations**: Adherence to transparency and disclosure requirements.
- **Custody and Security Measures**: Ensuring the secure handling of tokens and customer funds.

Example: The New York State Department of Financial Services (NYDFS) BitLicense, required for operating a crypto exchange in New York.

Cross-Border Considerations

Tokenization often involves cross-border transactions, necessitating an understanding of international laws.

- **Jurisdictional Challenges**: Compliance with laws of multiple jurisdictions where tokens are offered.
- **Tax Considerations**: Understanding tax liabilities in various countries.
- **Data Protection and Privacy Laws:** Adherence to international data privacy regulations.

Example: The General Data Protection Regulation (GDPR) in the European Union impacts data handling in tokenized systems.

Ethical and Social Considerations

Beyond legal compliance, ethical considerations play a vital role.

- **Sustainability and Environmental Concerns**: Addressing the ecological impact of blockchain technology.
- **Accessibility and Inclusion**: Ensuring that tokenization does not exclude underserved populations.
- **Transparency and Good Governance**: Upholding high ethical standards in token operations.

Example: Ethereum's transition to a Proof of Stake (PoS) model (ETH 2.0) addresses environmental concerns related to energy consumption.

Conclusion

The legal and regulatory considerations in tokenization form a multifaceted and dynamic aspect of this evolving field. From the legal classification of tokens to the intricate compliance requirements, this subchapter has illuminated the complexities of navigating the legal landscape of tokenized assets.

Through real-world examples and in-depth analysis, we've explored the essential legal dimensions of tokenization, highlighting the need for diligence, understanding, and foresight.

4.9 Practical Implementations of Tokenization in Various Industries

Tokenization has transcended the boundaries of cryptocurrency and has found its place in various industries. This subchapter explores how tokenization is revolutionizing different sectors, enabling new business models, enhancing efficiency, and fostering innovation.

Tokenization in Real Estate

Real estate is one of the most prominent fields benefiting from tokenization.

- **Fractional Ownership**: Tokenization enables fractional ownership, allowing more people to invest in property.
- **Liquidity Enhancement**: Tokens can be traded on secondary markets, increasing liquidity.
- **Transparency and Security**: Blockchain technology ensures a transparent and secure transaction process.

Example: Myco, a platform that offers tokenized real estate investments, enabling people to invest in properties with smaller capital.

Tokenization in Finance

Financial services are being reshaped by tokenization.

- **Asset-backed Securities**: Tokenizing traditional securities like bonds and stocks.

- **Decentralized Finance (DeFi):** Facilitating lending, borrowing, and trading through decentralized platforms.
- **Risk Management:** Creating more transparent and efficient risk assessment models.

Example: Compound, a DeFi platform that allows users to earn interest on their cryptocurrencies through tokenized lending protocols.

Tokenization in Art and Collectibles

The art world has embraced tokenization, especially with the rise of Non-Fungible Tokens (NFTs).

- **Democratizing Art Ownership**: NFTs allow artists to tokenize their work, enabling fractional ownership.
- **Provenance Tracking**: Tokenization ensures the authenticity and history of an artwork.
- **New Revenue Streams**: Artists can encode royalties into tokens, ensuring ongoing revenue.

Example: Beeple's digital artwork tokenized as an NFT and sold at Christie's for $69 million.

Tokenization in Supply Chain Management

Tokenization improves supply chain efficiency and traceability.

- **Real-time Tracking:** Tokenizing products allows real-time tracking throughout the supply chain.
- **Fraud Prevention**: Blockchain ensures the authenticity of products, minimizing counterfeiting.
- **Smart Contracts**: Automating contractual obligations using tokenized agreements.

Example: De Beers' use of blockchain to track the journey of diamonds, ensuring ethical sourcing and authenticity.

Tokenization in Healthcare

Healthcare sees significant promise in tokenization.

- **Secure Data Sharing**: Tokenization ensures the privacy and security of patient data.
- **Clinical Trials Management**: Enhancing the efficiency and integrity of clinical trials.
- **Medical Research Collaboration**: Facilitating secure and transparent cross-border collaborations.

Example: MedRec, a system using blockchain to manage medical records, enhancing accessibility and privacy.

Tokenization in Energy

Energy markets can benefit from tokenization as well.

- **Green Energy Trading**: Tokenizing renewable energy credits to facilitate green energy trading.
- **Grid Management**: Managing energy distribution through tokenized incentives and automation.
- **Energy Efficiency**: Encouraging energy-saving practices through token rewards.

Example: Power Ledger, a platform for peer-to-peer renewable energy trading, using tokenization to incentivize and manage transactions.

Conclusion

Subchapter 4.9 has provided a panoramic view of the practical implementations of tokenization across a spectrum of industries. From real estate to art, from finance to healthcare, the versatility and power of tokenization are evident.

With illustrative examples and in-depth analysis, we have unraveled the transformative potential of tokenization, demonstrating how it's not just a theoretical concept but a pragmatic solution reshaping industry.

4.10 Challenges and Limitations of Tokenization

While tokenization presents numerous opportunities and has found diverse applications across industries, it is not devoid of challenges and limitations. This subchapter takes a critical look at the difficulties that need to be overcome, the potential risks involved, and the areas where tokenization may have limitations.

Technical Challenges

Tokenization involves complex technologies, and the associated technical challenges are substantial.

- **Scalability Issues**: Many blockchain platforms face issues with handling a large number of transactions efficiently.
- **Interoperability Concerns**: Integration with existing systems and compatibility between different blockchain platforms.
- **Security Vulnerabilities**: Despite the inherent security of blockchain, smart contract flaws and other weaknesses can be exploited.

Example: The infamous DAO hack, where a flaw in a smart contract led to a loss of $60 million worth of Ether.

Regulatory and Legal Challenges

The regulatory landscape is a significant obstacle to tokenization.

- **Lack of Clear Regulation**: Ambiguity in laws can create uncertainty for businesses.
- **Cross-Border Legal Complexity**: Compliance with varying regulations across different jurisdictions.
- **Consumer Protection Concerns**: Ensuring that tokenized products meet legal standards for protecting consumers.

Example: The SEC's legal action against Ripple for the alleged unregistered securities offering of XRP tokens.

Market and Adoption Challenges

The adoption of tokenization faces market-related challenges.

- **Market Maturity**: The tokenization market is still relatively new, leading to uncertainties.
- **Lack of Standardization**: Different standards and practices can hinder widespread adoption.

- **Trust and Perception Issues**: Public perception and lack of trust in tokenized systems.

Example: The reluctance of traditional financial institutions to fully embrace DeFi due to concerns over regulation and security.

Ethical and Social Challenges

Tokenization also raises ethical and social concerns.

- **Accessibility and Inequality**: Ensuring that tokenization does not create or exacerbate economic inequality.
- **Environmental Impact**: Concerns over the energy consumption of certain blockchain platforms.
- **Privacy Concerns**: Balancing the transparency of blockchain with the need for privacy.

Example: Bitcoin's energy consumption, which has raised environmental concerns, leading to calls for more sustainable alternatives.

Limitations in Application

Tokenization may not be suitable for all scenarios.

- **Not a One-Size-Fits-All Solution**: Tokenization may not be appropriate for all types of assets or industries.
- **Potential Overcomplexity**: In some cases, traditional systems may be more efficient.
- **High Initial Costs**: The cost of implementing tokenization might be prohibitive for smaller businesses.

Conclusion

Subchapter 4.10 has offered a nuanced perspective on the challenges and limitations of tokenization, emphasizing that the path to innovation is often fraught with obstacles. From technical difficulties to regulatory hurdles, from market barriers to ethical dilemmas, the complexities of tokenization have been laid bare.

Through concrete examples and meticulous analysis, we have delved into the intricacies of the challenges faced in the tokenization landscape. This sobering look does not diminish the potential of tokenization but rather illuminates the need for thoughtful, responsible, and strategic implementation.

4.11 Future Trends and Developments in Tokenization

Tokenization is a dynamic and rapidly evolving field. As technology progresses, so do the possibilities for how tokenization can be applied and refined. In subchapter 4.11, we will explore the future trends and developments that are expected to shape the landscape of tokenization, setting the stage for the next wave of innovation.

Advancements in Technology

Technology drives the future, and tokenization is no exception.

- **Quantum-Resistant Cryptography**: Preparing for quantum computing by developing secure cryptographic algorithms.

- **Layer 2 Solutions**: Enhancing scalability through solutions like Lightning Network and Plasma.
- **Artificial Intelligence Integration**: Using AI to optimize tokenization processes and automate decision-making.

Example: StarkWare's use of zero-knowledge proofs (ZKPs) for scalability, allowing thousands of transactions per second on the Ethereum blockchain.

Regulatory Evolution

Changes in regulations will have a profound impact on tokenization's future.

- **Global Regulatory Harmonization**: Efforts to align regulations across countries to facilitate cross-border activities.
- **Clearer Guidelines**: Governments providing clearer regulations to promote growth and protect consumers.
- **Self-Regulation and Industry Standards**: Development of industry standards and self-regulatory organizations.

Example: The European Union's Markets in Crypto-assets (MiCA) regulation, aiming to create a harmonized framework for crypto-assets across member states.

Emerging Use Cases

New and innovative applications of tokenization will continue to emerge.

- **Tokenization of Intangible Assets**: Including intellectual property, reputation, and even social capital.
- **Community Ownership Models**: Facilitating community-driven development and governance through tokenization.
- **Tokenization in Government Services**: Using tokens to improve transparency and efficiency in public services.

Example: The city of Seoul's blockchain-based system for transparent management of public services.

Growth in Decentralized Finance (DeFi)

DeFi is expected to grow and evolve, driven by tokenization.

- **More Sophisticated Financial Products**: Creation of new tokenized financial instruments and derivatives.
- **Integration with Traditional Finance**: Bridging the gap between DeFi and traditional financial institutions.
- **Global Financial Inclusion**: Leveraging DeFi to provide financial services to unbanked populations.

Example: Uniswap, a decentralized exchange, paving the way for more advanced decentralized trading platforms.

Environmental Considerations

Sustainability and environmental impact will be key considerations.

- **Green Blockchain Technologies**: Development of more energy-efficient consensus algorithms.
- **Tokenization for Environmental Causes**: Using tokens to incentivize and fund environmental projects.

Example: Tezos using Proof-of-Stake (PoS), a more energy-efficient consensus mechanism, as an alternative to energy-intensive Proof-of-Work (PoW).

Conclusion

Subchapter 4.11 has provided a glimpse into the exciting future of tokenization. From technological advancements to regulatory evolution, from emerging use cases to the growth of DeFi, the landscape of tokenization is ripe for transformation.

With thoughtful insights and forward-thinking examples, we have navigated the potential pathways that tokenization may follow. The horizons of innovation are broad, and the opportunities are immense.

4.12 Practical Considerations in Tokenizing Assets

Tokenizing assets is not a mere theoretical concept; it's a practical process that requires careful planning, clear understanding, and meticulous execution. In subchapter 4.12, we will navigate through the essential practical considerations that will guide the reader in the tokenization journey. From selecting the right technology to ensuring legal compliance, from building a robust security framework to engaging stakeholders, this section covers it all.

Choosing the Right Technology

Selecting the appropriate technology is crucial for successful tokenization.

- **Assessing Platform Capabilities**: Understanding the technological features, scalability, and interoperability of different blockchain platforms.

- **Alignment with Business Goals**: Choosing technology that aligns with the specific needs and objectives of the tokenization project.

Example: Selecting Ethereum for an ERC-20 token due to its widespread adoption and robust smart contract capabilities.

Ensuring Legal and Regulatory Compliance

Compliance is paramount in tokenization.

- **Understanding Jurisdictional Regulations**: Being aware of the legal requirements and regulations in the jurisdiction where the token will be issued.
- **Engaging Legal Experts**: Working with legal professionals specializing in blockchain and tokenization.

Example: Ensuring that a tokenized real estate asset complies with local property laws and securities regulations.

Developing a Security Framework

Security is at the heart of any tokenization project.

- **Implementing Robust Security Protocols**: Protecting against unauthorized access, fraud, and cyberattacks.
- **Periodic Security Audits**: Regular assessments by external security experts to identify and mitigate vulnerabilities.

Example: Implementing multi-signature wallets to enhance the security of tokenized assets.

Engaging with Stakeholders

Stakeholder engagement is essential for a successful tokenization project.

- **Clear Communication and Transparency**: Regularly communicating with stakeholders, including investors, regulators, and the community.

- **Building Trust and Credibility**: Demonstrating commitment to ethical practices, transparency, and compliance.

Example: Creating a transparent and comprehensive whitepaper for a tokenized project to inform potential investors and stakeholders.

Evaluating Market Dynamics

Understanding the market landscape is crucial.

- **Market Research and Analysis**: Assessing the demand, competition, and potential challenges in the market.
- **Positioning and Differentiation**: Finding a unique value proposition that sets the tokenized asset apart.

Example: Assessing the demand for tokenized art in the current market landscape to determine the feasibility of an art tokenization project.

Ethical Considerations

Ethical considerations should not be overlooked.

- **Ensuring Fair Practices**: Implementing mechanisms to prevent fraudulent activities and protect investor rights.
- **Social Responsibility**: Considering the societal impact and ensuring that the project aligns with broader social values.

Example: Ensuring that a tokenized environmental project genuinely contributes to sustainability and does not engage in "greenwashing."

Conclusion

Subchapter 4.12 has offered a practical roadmap for anyone looking to embark on the journey of tokenizing assets. It has provided a comprehensive view of the multifaceted considerations that must be addressed, each with its importance and complexity.

Through illustrative examples and concrete guidance, this section has illuminated the path from concept to execution, underscoring the importance of planning, compliance, security, engagement, market insight, and ethics.

4.13 Risks and Challenges in Tokenizing Assets

Tokenization offers incredible opportunities, but it is not without its share of risks and challenges. In subchapter 4.13, we will dissect the potential pitfalls, hurdles, and complexities that may arise in the process of tokenizing assets. From technical difficulties to regulatory uncertainties, from market risks to ethical dilemmas, this section provides a comprehensive overview, equipping the reader with the knowledge to navigate these challenges successfully.

Technical Risks

The technical landscape of tokenization is intricate, and several risks may arise.

- **Smart Contract Vulnerabilities**: Bugs or flaws in smart contracts can lead to losses or unauthorized actions.
- **Scalability Issues**: Limitations in handling a large number of transactions may affect performance.
- **Interoperability Challenges**: Difficulties in seamless integration between different blockchain platforms.

Example: The DAO hack, where a vulnerability in a smart contract led to the loss of $50 million worth of Ether.

Regulatory and Legal Risks

Legal and regulatory compliance is complex and poses significant risks.

- **Regulatory Uncertainty**: Changing or unclear regulations may create compliance challenges.
- **Legal Disputes**: Potential legal conflicts related to ownership, rights, or contractual obligations.

- **Jurisdictional Complexities**: Differences in regulations across various jurisdictions can complicate cross-border activities.

Example: The SEC's legal actions against some Initial Coin Offerings (ICOs) for non-compliance with securities laws.

Market Risks

Market dynamics present their unique set of challenges.

- **Market Volatility**: Fluctuations in the value of tokens can affect investors and the overall stability of the project.
- **Liquidity Issues**: Difficulties in buying or selling tokens without significantly affecting their price.
- **Competitive Pressures**: The rapidly evolving competitive landscape may affect the project's success.

Example: The decline in value of utility tokens due to market saturation or reduced demand.

Security Risks

The digital nature of tokenization brings about potential security threats.

- **Cyberattacks**: Potential hacks, phishing, or other malicious activities targeting the tokenized assets.
- **Insider Threats**: Malicious actions from within the organization, such as fraud or theft.
- **Data Privacy Concerns**: Risks related to the handling and protection of sensitive personal data.

Example: The Mt. Gox hack, where a Bitcoin exchange was hacked, leading to the loss of 850,000 Bitcoins.

Ethical and Social Risks

Ethical considerations also present potential challenges.

- **Social Impact Concerns**: Potential negative impacts on communities or the environment.

- **Transparency and Trust Issues**: Lack of transparency may erode trust among stakeholders.

Example: A project tokenizing natural resources without considering the impact on local communities.

Conclusion

Subchapter 4.13 has been a deep dive into the multifaceted risks and challenges that accompany the tokenization journey. Recognizing and addressing these challenges is not merely a matter of compliance or risk mitigation; it is an essential part of responsible innovation.

Through careful examination, practical examples, and clear articulation of complexities, this section equips the reader to approach tokenization with a keen awareness of potential pitfalls and the tools to navigate them successfully.

Solar Energy Tokenization Project

In this case, we will develop a solar energy tokenization project for existing solar energy production plants. This project will allow these plants to tokenize their energy production and allow investors to buy and sell these tokens. The data I will provide is fictitious but based on real statistics to provide a realistic example.

Research and Planning

First, it's important to understand how much energy existing solar power plants produce and how much they could earn by selling this energy. For our example, we will consider a solar power plant in Phoenix, Arizona. According to data from Solar.com, residential solar panels have an efficiency of 20% on average. In Phoenix, there is an average of 5 peak sunlight hours per day. The plant we are considering is 1 MW in size.

Considering the efficiency of the panels and the peak sunlight hours, we can estimate that the plant produces approximately 1000 kWh of energy per day. At a selling price of $0.08 per kWh (which is the price some home producers get for selling energy back to the grid), the plant could earn $80 a day selling its energy.

Development of the Blockchain Platform

1.1 Choice of Blockchain

For this project, we decided to use Ethereum due to its popularity, support for smart contracts, and widespread adoption in the cryptocurrency market. Although Ethereum's transaction fees can be high (around $0.87 per transaction on average), its broad adoption and the availability of development infrastructure make it a reasonable choice.

1.2 Protocol Development

The protocol for the blockchain platform will consist of an ERC20 token and a set of smart contracts that will allow solar power plants to issue tokens in proportion to the amount of energy they produce and burn tokens when they sell this energy.

Each token will represent 1 kWh of solar energy produced. Thus, if the plant produces 1000 kWh of energy a day, it will issue 1000 tokens per day. When it sells this energy back to the grid for $80, it will burn the corresponding 1000 tokens.

Investors will be able to buy and sell these tokens on a secondary market. In this way, they can invest in solar energy production and benefit from fluctuations in the price of this energy.

1.3 Smart Contract Development

The necessary smart contracts for this project will be:

- A contract for the ERC20 token, which will include functions to mint and burn tokens.
- A contract for the secondary market, which will allow investors to buy and sell tokens.
- A contract for the solar power plant, which will interact with the token contract to mint tokens when the plant produces energy and burn tokens when it sells this energy.

We have already covered the research and planning, the choice of blockchain, and the development of smart contracts.

Project Implementation

2.1 Installation of Measurement Equipment

To carry out this project, we will need to install measurement equipment at the participating solar plants. These devices will be responsible for measuring energy production and transmitting this data to the blockchain platform.

For instance, we could install smart meters that can communicate directly with our blockchain platform. These meters would need to be compatible with IoT (Internet of Things) technology and be able to accurately record the amount of solar energy produced.

2.2 Integration of Measurement Equipment with the Blockchain Platform

Once the measurement equipment is installed, we would need to develop an interface that allows these devices to interact with our blockchain platform. This might involve the creation of custom software or firmware that can securely and efficiently transmit solar energy production data to the blockchain platform.

For example, we could develop software that runs on the smart meters and transmits the solar energy production data to the blockchain platform every time a certain amount of energy is produced (e.g., every 1 kWh produced).

2.3 Testing and Commissioning

After the measurement systems are integrated with the blockchain platform, we should conduct a series of tests to ensure everything is working correctly. This could include conducting solar energy production tests and verifying that tokens are issued and burned appropriately.

Once we are confident that the system is operating correctly, we could start deploying it to the participating solar plants. Each solar plant that joins the project would receive a certain number of tokens based on its solar energy production.

2.4 Development of a User Interface

To allow users to interact with the system, we would need to develop a user-friendly interface. This interface would enable users to buy and sell solar energy tokens, as well as view real-time information on solar energy production.

For instance, we could develop a web or mobile application that allows users to buy and sell solar energy tokens and view real-time information about the solar energy production of the participating solar plants.

Operation and Maintenance

3.1 Monitoring Solar Energy Production

Once the system is up and running, continuous monitoring of the solar energy production of participating plants will be essential. This will allow us to issue and burn tokens accurately, as well as detect any issues that may arise.

For instance, we could implement an alert system that notifies us if a solar plant's energy production falls below a certain threshold. We might also use machine learning technology to predict solar energy production and adjust token issuance accordingly.

3.2 Maintenance of the Blockchain Platform

Like any other software system, our blockchain platform will require regular maintenance. This could include updating smart contracts, implementing new features, and addressing any issues that might emerge.

For example, we might need to update smart contracts to incorporate new features, such as the ability to sell solar energy tokens to other energy grids. We might also need to address security or performance issues that arise.

3.3 User Support

Finally, we'll need to provide support to the users of our platform. This could encompass resolving technical issues, assisting with token transactions, and educating on how to use our platform.

For instance, we could implement a customer support system that allows users to submit support tickets if they encounter any issues. We might also develop educational materials, like video tutorials and blog articles, to help users understand how to use our platform.

Expansion

Once the system is operational and has a track record of success, we could consider expanding it to other forms of renewable energy, such as wind or hydroelectric power. This would allow more renewable energy producers to benefit from tokenizing their energy production and would also provide users with a broader range of renewable energy investment options.

For example, we might develop additional smart contracts to tokenize wind or hydroelectric power production. We could also seek partnerships with renewable energy producers in other parts of the world to expand our platform globally.

Minimum Necessary Smart Contracts

The design of smart contracts largely depends on the specific needs of the system you are creating. That said, for a system that tokenizes solar energy production, you might need the following smart contracts and the associated functions and events:

- **Solar Panel Ownership Contract (SolarPanelOwnershipContract):** This contract could represent the ownership of individual solar panels.
- **transferOwnership**: This function would allow the transfer of ownership of a solar panel from one user to another.
- **Event OwnershipTransferred**: This event would be emitted when ownership of a solar panel is transferred.
- **Energy Production Contract (EnergyProductionContract):** This contract would keep track of the energy production of each solar panel.

- **recordEnergyProduction**: This function would allow recording the energy production of a solar panel at a given time.
- **Event EnergyProduced**: This event would be emitted each time energy production is recorded.
- **Energy Token Contract (EnergyTokenContract)**: This contract would represent the energy tokens that are issued based on energy production.
- **mint**: This function would allow for the creation of new energy tokens, probably called in conjunction with recordEnergyProduction.
- **transfer**: This function would allow the transfer of energy tokens from one user to another.
- **Event TokensMinted**: This event would be emitted when new energy tokens are minted.
- **Event TokensTransferred**: This event would be emitted when energy tokens are transferred.
- **Energy Sale Contract (EnergySaleContract)**: This contract would handle the sale of energy (or energy tokens) to the grid or other users.

- **sellEnergy**: This function would allow a user to sell their energy to the grid or another user.
- **Event EnergySold**: This event would be emitted when energy is sold.

These are just examples of the contracts, functions, and events you might need. Depending on the exact details of your system, you might need additional contracts or different functions and events. It's also important to consider that these contracts would need a set of auxiliary functions to manage aspects such as user authentication, error handling, and compliance with business rules.

Here's an example of smart contracts that could be used for a solar energy tokenization system. Smart contracts will be implemented in Solidity, which is a programming language for smart contracts on the Ethereum network.

Solar Energy Contract (SolarEnergyContract): This contract would be responsible for issuing and burning tokens based on the production and sale of solar energy.

```solidity
pragma solidity ^0.8.0;

import "@openzeppelin/contracts/token/ERC20/ERC20.sol";

contract SolarEnergyContract is ERC20 {

    address public owner;

    mapping (address => uint256) public energyBalance;

    // Events

    event EnergyProduced(address indexed producer, uint256 amount);

    event EnergyConsumed(address indexed consumer, uint256 amount);

    constructor() ERC20("SolarEnergyToken", "SET") {

        owner = msg.sender;

    }

    modifier onlyOwner() {
```

```
        require(owner == msg.sender, "Only
the owner can call this function.");

        _;

    }

    function produceEnergy(address producer,
uint256 amount) external onlyOwner {

        _mint(producer, amount); // Issues
SET tokens to the producer

        energyBalance[producer] += amount;

        emit EnergyProduced(producer,
amount); // Emits an energy produced event

    }

    function consumeEnergy(address consumer,
uint256 amount) external {

        require(balanceOf(consumer) >=
amount, "You don't have enough SET tokens.");

        _burn(consumer, amount); // Burns SET
tokens from the consumer

        energyBalance[consumer] -= amount;

        emit EnergyConsumed(consumer,
amount); // Emits an energy consumed event

    }

}
```

This contract assumes that each solar energy producer has an associated Ethereum address and that the contract owner can call the produceEnergy function to issue SET tokens to the producer each time they produce energy. Energy consumers can burn their SET tokens by calling the consumeEnergy function.

Solar Panel Ownership Contract (SolarPanelOwnershipContract): This contract would keep a record of the ownership of solar panels.

```solidity
pragma solidity ^0.8.0;

contract SolarPanelOwnershipContract {

    struct SolarPanel {

        address owner;

        uint256 panelId;

    }

    SolarPanel[] public solarPanels;

    // Events

    event OwnershipTransferred(uint256 indexed panelId, address indexed oldOwner, address indexed newOwner);
```

```
    function transferOwnership(uint256 
panelId, address newOwner) external {

        SolarPanel storage panel = 
solarPanels[panelId];

        require(msg.sender == panel.owner, 
"Only the current owner can transfer 
ownership.");

        address oldOwner = panel.owner;

        panel.owner = newOwner;

        emit OwnershipTransferred(panelId, 
oldOwner, newOwner); // Emits an ownership 
transfer event

    }

}
```

This contract allows solar panel owners to transfer ownership to another Ethereum address. Each time ownership is transferred, an OwnershipTransferred event is emitted.

These are simplified examples and do not account for all possible complications and security considerations. In a real system, it would be necessary to implement additional security measures, such as the use of access contracts, and you might also want to implement additional functions.

If we want to include a mechanism to automatically handle the production and consumption of energy, we could introduce an EnergyProducer contract and an EnergyConsumer contract. Here are some basic examples:

EnergyMaker Contract: This contract supervises the generation of energy and spontaneously creates tokens when energy is made.

```
pragma solidity ^0.5.16;

import "./SolarEnergyToken.sol";

contract EnergyMaker {

    SolarEnergyToken public tokenInstance;

    mapping(address => uint256) public totalEnergyGenerated;

    event EnergyGenerated(address indexed generator, uint256 quantity);

    constructor(SolarEnergyToken _tokenInstance) public {
```

```
        tokenInstance = _tokenInstance;

    }

    function generateEnergy(uint256 quantity) public {

        totalEnergyGenerated[msg.sender] += quantity;

        tokenInstance.mint(msg.sender, quantity);

        emit EnergyGenerated(msg.sender, quantity);

    }

}
```

Within this contract, generateEnergy is a function that a generator uses upon energy generation. It updates the totalEnergyGenerated mapping and bestows new tokens to the generator.

EnergyUser Contract: This contract oversees the utilization of energy and systematically deducts tokens during energy usage.

```
pragma solidity ^0.5.16;

import "./SolarEnergyToken.sol";
```

```solidity
contract EnergyUser {

    SolarEnergyToken public tokenInstance;

    mapping(address => uint256) public totalEnergyUsed;

    event EnergyUsed(address indexed user, uint256 quantity);

    constructor(SolarEnergyToken _tokenInstance) public {

        tokenInstance = _tokenInstance;

    }

    function useEnergy(uint256 quantity) public {

        require(tokenInstance.balanceOf(msg.sender) >= quantity, "Insufficient tokens to use energy");

        totalEnergyUsed[msg.sender] += quantity;

        tokenInstance.burn(msg.sender, quantity);

        emit EnergyUsed(msg.sender, quantity);

    }

}
```

In this contract, useEnergy is an action that a user initiates when they utilize energy. The function updates the totalEnergyUsed mapping and eliminates tokens from the user's balance.

It's worth noting that the aforementioned are just rudimentary representations. In a genuine system, supplementary attributes like fee administration, penalties for exceeding consumption or not reaching the production target, incentives for additional generation, and so forth would be incorporated. Moreover, the generation and utilization of energy would probably be gauged by IoT apparatuses, and this data would be transmitted to the blockchain autonomously. Consequently, crafting a secure methodology for IoT gadgets to interface with the blockchain would be imperative.

Monetization of a Tokenization Project

There are several ways to monetize this type of project. Here are some:

- **Transaction Fees**: You could charge a small fee for each transaction made on the platform. This fee could be in the form of a small number of tokens that would be deducted from each transaction. This method is common in many token and cryptocurrency platforms.
- **Premium Services**: You could offer additional services for a fee. For instance, you could provide data analysis, energy production forecasts, energy optimization recommendations, consulting services, and so on.
- **Token Sales**: As the platform gains users and the demand for tokens increases, the value of the tokens can rise. You could retain a number of tokens to sell them later when their value has increased.

- **Advertising**: If the platform has a large user base, you could make money through advertising. You could allow solar energy companies and other related businesses to advertise their products and services on the platform.
- **Partnerships**: You could partner with solar energy companies, equipment manufacturers, and other industry players to offer joint services or products. These companies might pay a fee for such partnerships.

Each of these methods has its own pros and cons, and the best choice will depend on the specific business model of the platform. It's important to note that any monetization method should align with the overall goal of the project and provide value to the platform's users.

AUTOR

MICHAEL CATHAL